Pacific People Sing Out Strong

Compiled and Edited by
William L. Coop

Friendship Press   New York

Friendship Press   **New York**

Library of Congress Cataloging in Publication Data
Main entry under title:

Pacific people sing out strong.

  1. Islands of the Pacific—Addresses, essays, lectures
 2. Christianity—Islands of the Pacific—Addresses, essays,
lectures. I. Coop, William L., 1938-
DU18.P25   261.8'0996   81-22211
ISBN: 0-377-00118-X   AACR2

Scripture quotations designated (TEV) are from the *Good
News Bible,* the Bible in Today's English Version. Copyright
© American Bible Society 1976.

Bible quotations from the Revised Standard Version, © 1946
and 1952 by the Division of Christian Education of the National Council of the Churches of Christ in the United States of
America, are used by permission.

**Editorial Office: 475 Riverside Drive, Room 772,
New York, NY 10115
Distribution Office: PO Box 37844, Cincinnati,
OH 45237**

Printed in the United States of America

A Psalm of the Pacific

Our Pacific islands are yours, O Lord,
And all the seas that surround them.
You made the palm trees grow,
And the birds fly in the air.

When we see your beautiful rising sun,
And hear the waves splash on our shores,
When we see the new moon rise
And the old moon sink,

We know, O Lord, how wonderful you are.
You bless our people;
From Truk to Tonga and beyond
You spread your caring wings.

Even when we sail through stormy seas,
And fly amidst rain clouds,
We know you await us,
With kaikai and coconut.

You who turn storms into gentle winds,
And troubled seas into tranquil waters,
You who make yams grow
And bananas blossom,

Wash our people with justice;
Teach us with righteousness;
Speak to us daily;
Strengthen us to serve you.

Bernard Narokobi

DESIGN ON DANCE SHIELD

Contents

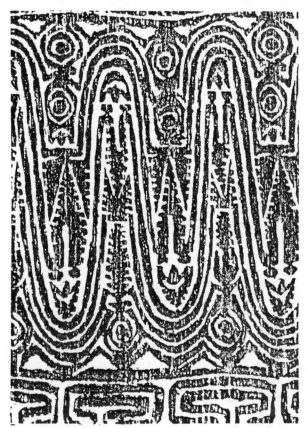

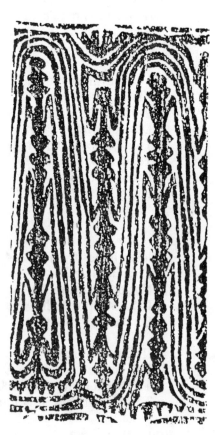

Preface

The South Pacific Islands region was first proposed as the geographic theme for mission study in 1982-83 because this area is an emerging frontier of church development. Eighty-five percent of the population of the islands is Christian. The intense pressure of Western culture, continuing colonial attitudes on the part of the United States and France and nuclear testing activities give cause for concern for the global future. What is challenging to us as American Christians is the activity of the churches, led by the vision of the Pacific Conference of Churches.

In this book we will encounter the movement among Pacific leaders to balance the richness of primal Pacific culture with the positive and negative intrusions of Western society. What impressed me most during the six years of our ministry in Vanuatu (formerly the New Hebrides), Papua New Guinea and Fiji was the constant vision of the emerging leadership in both church and nation-state, buttressing their people's religious dedication and their yearnings to be free.

Pacific People Sing Out Strong. This choice of title is significant. In 1982 the words are sung out by those who just ten years ago were singing a vision amid great colonial restraints in both church and government. But great change has come — change that even the most visionary singers were expecting only for the 1990s or perhaps by the year 2000. For example, in early 1972, the colonial administration in Papua and New Guinea was predicting independence for the mid-80s. On September 15, 1975, Papua New Guinea celebrated Independence Day. In 1974 the French and British administrations in the New Hebrides were annoyed by the emergence of a National Pati (party) and by the "upstart" Presbyterian and Anglican Assemblies' call for movement toward self-government and eventual independence; on July 31, 1980, Vanuatu celebrated Independence Day.

Of the seventeen nation-states which make up the islands of the South Pacific, five received their full independence between 1974 and 1980. They join the five already independent from the 1960s and look toward the movement of France and the United States in the remaining seven crucial areas—crucial because France and the United States label these areas (French Polynesia, New Caledonia and the U.S. Trust Territories) as "strategic."

"The Challenges of the 80s and the Mission of the Pacific Churches" was the theme of the Fourth Assembly of the Pacific Conference of Churches, held in Tonga in 1981. The major contents of this scrapbook are the preparation papers for the Fourth Assembly. We have the unique privilege of wrestling along with the member churches of the PCC over their agenda for the 1980s. This agenda is ours as well as theirs because of our global interdependence, so I ask you to hear Pacific people as they *Sing Out Strong*.

Each section of the book will be prefaced by a note from the editor introducing the speakers you will encounter. The poetry and songs that separate the articles lend a scrapbook flavor to these pages. Song and dance and poetic storytelling are important to Pacific people. The informal time around the fire or at the "sing-sing" (song and dance competition) is most important for serious decision making in the village. And when the village voice is heard, that is the time when we can truly hear the Pacific people sing out strong.

Bill Coop

PART ONE:

ABOUT THIS BOOK

Editor's Note: The poem "A Psalm of the Pacific" is a fitting prayer with which to open this book. No meeting in the Pacific Islands begins, it seems, without a prayer. Bernard Narokobi from Papua New Guinea is a lawyer, past member of the Supreme Court, author of the Constitution of Papua New Guinea and now has returned to his village to make sense out of the struggles of the 1970s for independence and village justice. Narokobi is a Catholic lay leader and a friend.

It is fitting that this book begin (after prayer) with a letter from Ms. Lorine Tevi, general secretary of the Pacific Conference of Churches (in January 1982 she began work with the education department of the World Council of Churches in Geneva). Her letter is followed by a statement from the Secretariat of the Pacific Conference of Churches that was sent out in February 1981 in preparation for the Fourth Assembly, held in May of that year. Since it is addressed to those directly involved and "all other interested persons," it makes an appropriate introduction for North American Christians to the issues, and to the resources of the Bible, prayer and faith, which are central to the thoughts and actions of our brothers and sisters of the Pacific Islands.

This section closes with a poem by Kumalau Tawali, a Papua New Guinea student, who catches the essence of nationalism and people's desires for dignity over against the categories that foreigners often impose.

B. David Williams, Jr.

United Methodist Board of Global Ministries by John C. Goodwin

1. Outdoor ecumenical service in Papua New Guinea features T-shirts with pidgin slogans.

2. A country church in Vanuatu.

3

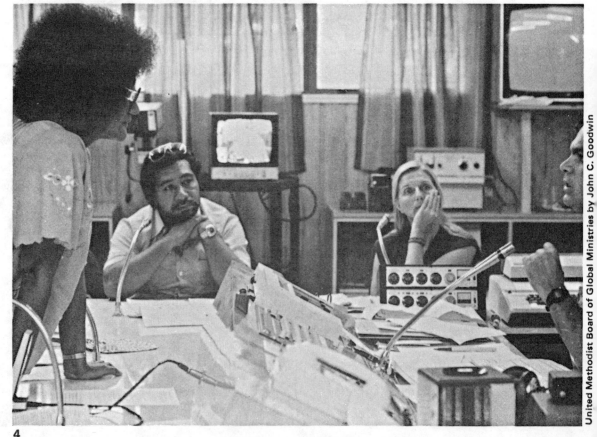

4

3. *Dr. S. Amanaki Havea, a well-known ecumenical leader from Tonga, speaks at the Fourth Assembly of the Pacific Conference of Churches.*

4. *The Satellite Center at the University of the South Pacific is used by the Pacific Conference of Churches.*

A Letter To Readers

B. David Williams, Jr.

Lorine Tevi

Pacific Conference of Churches
P.O. Box 208
Suva, Fiji

Dear Sisters and Brothers in Christ,

To our partners and friends in the region and in the rest of the world who are interested in what is happening in the Pacific from the point of view of indigenous writers and the Pacific churches: we pray that you will find this book interesting and helpful. Many of the offerings in this scrapbook were prepared for the Fourth Assembly of the Pacific Conference of Churches held in May, 1981, at Nuku'alofa, Tonga. The remaining poetry and presentations were taken from conferences and events sponsored by the Pacific Conference of Churches between 1978 and 1980. All intend to show the concerns and feelings of Pacific peoples as they prepare for the challenge of the 1980s.

When writers were approached during the early stages of planning for the Assembly, we thanked God that individuals in the region were able to meet our needs. As they addressed themselves to the theme, "The Challenges of the 80s and the Mission of the Pacific Churches," there emerged a collection of insights into today's Pacific reality. We are thankful that most of these writers are indigenous Pacific Islanders, expressing themselves in their present state of development from the "old to the new Pacific."

May this book deepen our understanding of the Pacific realities and may it challenge our faith in a living God. Join us in our study, biblical reflection and prayerful action as we approach the challenge of the 1980s together.

Lorine Tevi
General Secretary

Editor's Note: *The new general secretary of the Pacific Conference of Churches, now beginning a five-year term, is the Reverend Baiteke Nabetari.*

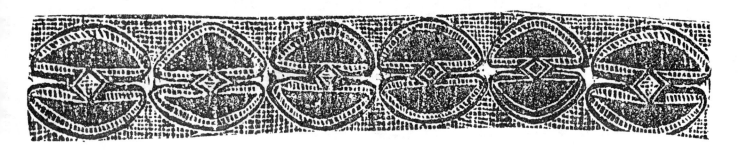

CONCERNING THE PACIFIC

TO: Pacific Conference of Churches Member Churches
Brother and Sister Christians Throughout the World
All Other Interested Persons
FROM: The Pacific Conference of Churches Secretariat

The Pacific as an Arena of Increasing Competition, Conflict and Struggle

The Pacific seems to live up to its name. It appears to be a peaceful place. Dramatic visible expressions of violence are not widely found. Yet in its own way the Pacific is rapidly becoming an arena of intense competition, conflict and struggle. Its eco-system is in danger of irreparable harm. Its cultures, rich in values, are being eroded, some of them undone. For those who view human life in its wholeness, who see humans in relation to their community and culture and in intimate relation to their ecological context, this raises fundamental human rights questions.

For some years we have been pressing eagerly toward the "de-colonization" of the Pacific. But it is becoming clear that even though many Pacific nations have their political independence, new kinds of colonialism are taking over, and with great force. Powerful countries, at the expense of the ocean and the islands, the people and the future of humanity, are thoughtlessly seeking to satisfy their insatiable hunger for material resources and for control; they would put away from their own shores their excretion of wastes; they increasingly use the Pacific space for self-serving military strategies which are dangerous and unthinkable, and which in the name of "security" leave the whole world trembling.

So we are concerned about the profound human rights implications in the attitude that the Pacific Ocean, its islands and its people may be used for narrow and selfish purposes by whoever have the brazen power to do so. At this moment we see this power wielded more in economic than military terms and exercised in ways more subtle than direct.

Let us consider the importance of a clean, peaceful, life-giving Pacific not only for the Pacific peoples, but for all humanity, now and in the generations to come! It appears that Pacific people must be the ones to speak out about this, on their own behalf and on behalf of all humankind.

We outline particular areas of concern, each one significant in itself, and all examples of the unfortunate attitude that the Pacific is an open frontier, fair game for those with the power to play:

Nuclear testing continues in French Polynesia in spite of the clearly and repeatedly stated wishes of the Pacific people. The French have reportedly tested nearly 80 nuclear devices at Mururoa. Reports that the land is subsiding, in some cases beneath the sea, and that cracks have appeared in the atoll, both on the surface and under water outside, give rise to grave concern. The only monitoring of the radioactive leakage into the sea is conducted by the French military, in strict secrecy.

The dumping of radioactive wastes poses a frightening threat to the Pacific Ocean and to future generations. We are told by concerned experts that a sound scientific basis does not yet exist for the safe disposal of radioactive wastes. Yet regular dumping of nuclear wastes in the Pacific appears imminent. "Experimental" dumping of low-level wastes will most likely begin during the coming year, with Japan, in collaboration with the United States, leading the way. Pacific people have consistently shown their sharp opposition. With the United States and the USSR included, there are at least 133 nuclear power stations in operation in seven countries on the Pacific rim,

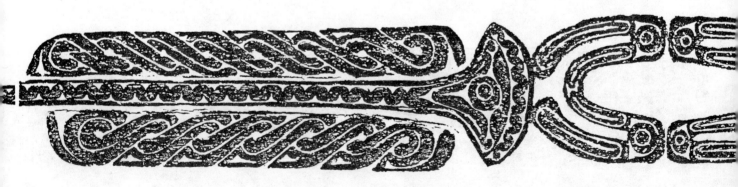

not counting India's three. More are planned or already under construction. These nuclear power stations produce dangerous amounts of radioactive wastes. The 1972 London Convention does not in fact serve as a safeguard for nuclear waste disposal, but as a license to dump. We note here the intimate relationship between nuclear power and nuclear weapons. We point out the danger of having more than 250 nuclear submarines in the world's oceans.

French colonial presence in the Pacific remains a serious concern. While the French reluctantly left Vanuatu (the new name for the New Hebrides upon independence in July 1980), the situation in mineral-rich New Caledonia is more complex and difficult. The prospect of violent confrontation is very real. As with Vanuatu, here we see a particularly unfortunate colonial history: from an estimated 200,000 persons before colonization, the Melanesian population had been reduced to about 27,000 by 1920, in brutally crushed revolts. While in recent years the Melanesian population has grown considerably, its growth has been countered through a French policy encouraging the immigration of non-Melanesians. So the indigenous population has now been systematically out-populated and marginalized, a process some people call "genocide by substitution." No situation in the Pacific calls for more immediate and sensitive attention than New Caledonia.

Fundamental human rights questions are raised in the way the United States has discharged its responsibilities for the Pacific Island Trust Territory. The United States was charged under the Trusteeship Agreement to "protect the inhabitants against the loss of their land or resources," and to "protect the health of the inhabitants." We hope that an impartial evaluation and a vigorous constructive debate may take place under the auspices of the United Nations to help clarify the basic relationships now being confirmed in Micronesia. We note in both the Commonwealth Covenant and the Compacts of Free Association that while they appear to give political autonomy, the United States has "discretion" so broad and ambiguous as to be virtually unlimited (especially in relation to the "incompatibility" exception mentioned in section 313 of the compacts). United States retention of major islands in the Marshalls for a missile range and apparent United States determination to establish a military base at Babeldaob, Belau, all being sought through clever economic enticements, reveal lack of commitment to the true self-determination and integrity of the Micronesian people. It is in Micronesia where we see most clearly that the buying and selling of rights has become the "new formula for self-reliance," an unfortunate pattern which is having tragic effect upon lifestyle. The dramatic youth suicide problem in Micronesia is surely in part a reflection of the cultural disintegration taking place.

While we appreciate Japan's rich culture and enjoy many fine products from Japan, her rise as economic imperial giant raises serious questions for the Pacific Island nations. The "Pacific Basin Cooperation Concept" (PBCC) being promoted by Japan with the ready support of the United States and Australia, and less enthusiastically by some others, represents an unfortunate reinforcement of existing relationships of power and control. Endorsement by the Pacific island nations is now being sought for the PBCC as a means of "legitimizing" the scheme in a psychological/political sense. The process is well-lubricated by a multitude of new aid offers. In 1980, for the first time in modern history, the value of trade carried in the Pacific exceeded that of the Atlantic, largely due to Japan. Globally, Japan is now first in steel, autos and electronics. In the name of "self-defense," Japan now assembles its own military planes and is manufacturing its own tanks. With 250 companies involved in military research and development, Japanese arms expertise is growing, and a fierce debate is now taking place as to whether or not under the "Peace Constitution" Japan may develop an armaments industry. This debate even involves whether or not Japan may make and possess nuclear weapons! With growing market limitations for its usual products, Japanese businessmen and workers' unions appear to be leaning in favor of producing arms for export. Is it unreasonable to expect that Japan will be deeply involved in the growing militarization of the Pacific?

There are other concerns. While not mentioned by name above, Australia, New Zealand and Canada all play a significant part in the commercialization, nuclearization and militarization of the Pacific. The unjust treatment of the indigenous people of the Pacific rim must be seen as an integral part of the greater concern which we are trying to express. The coming of deep-seabed mining brings a new kind of competition and unknown dangers for the ocean, with the benefits to Pacific people as yet very unclear. Many Pacific countries are strongly attractive to tourists, yet we have a limited capacity to absorb them without serious effect upon our way of life. Resort tourism is having major impact upon political and economic decisions in some of our countries. As in many other parts of the world, transnational corporations wield great influence in the Pacific, and while they provide us with desirable products and services, to whom are they accountable? What effect are they having upon our Pacific identity and our own capacity to do and to make? Our difficult and complex land questions are very much affected by outside forces. Land questions will eventually shake most Pacific island countries to their very roots!

The forces now determining the direction of the lives of Pacific people come largely from outside. They may seem impersonal in nature, but they represent collective vested interests of very real persons and groups. We recognize that sometimes Pacific people and their leaders unwittingly become allies of these undesirable forces. We are often too easygoing, too comfortable, not critical enough about what is happening to us. Sometimes we are more interested in the "progress" of members of our own family than in the well-being of our country and region.

We ask our Pacific Island people and leaders to join in working for a clearer understanding among Pacific people of what is happening in this region; for critical self-examination; for a clarification of national and regional goals; for a reaffirmation of Pacific values.

We appeal to brother and sister Christians of nations having such strong influence over what is happening in our region to join with us in working for a more enlightened political will and a stronger accountability to the world for what is being done in the Pacific.

We urge that concerned persons everywhere press for responsible continuing debate and action in the United Nations at every appropriate level on these and all questions concerning the Pacific as an arena of increasing injustice.

Biblical/Theological Reflections in Relation to Pacific Issues, Under the Themes: Stewardship, Justice and Peacemaking

Concerning Stewardship

We have a solemn responsibility to care for the universe which God has created, and for the many expressions of God-given life which it contains and supports. For this we are accountable to God, to each other and to future generations.

> Then God said, "And now we will make human beings; they will be like us and resemble us. They will have power over the fish, the birds, and all animals, domestic and wild, large and small." So God created human beings, making them to be like himself. He created them male and female, blessed them, and said, "Have many children, so that your descendants will live all over the earth and bring it under their control. I am putting you in charge...." (Genesis 1:26-28a, TEV)

> When I look at the sky, which you have made, at the moon and the stars, which you set in their places—what is man, that you think of him; mere man, that you care for him? Yet you made him inferior only to yourself; you crowned him with glory and honor. You appointed him ruler over everything you made; you placed him over all creation: sheep and cattle, and the wild animals too; the birds and the fish and the creatures in the seas. (Psalm 8:3-8, TEV)

"Stewardship" implies that we live in a limited world. Although we human beings are "made in God's image," we are limited in our cleverness. As our capacities expand, we must learn to deal humbly and responsibly at every stage with our limitations. The earth is also limited. It is limited in its capacity to suffer exploitation. It is entirely possible for us human beings to hurt seriously the world in which we live.

> Much is required from the person to whom much is given; much more is required from the person to whom much more is given. (Adapted from Luke 12:48b)

> Whoever is faithful in small matters will be faithful in large ones; whoever is dishonest in small matters will be dishonest in large ones. If, then, you have not been faithful in handling worldly wealth, how can you be trusted with true wealth? And if you have not been faithful with what belongs to someone else, who will give you what belongs to you? (Luke 16:10-12, TEV)

> Each one, as a good manager of God's different gifts, must use for the good of others the special gift he has received from God. (1 Peter 4:10, TEV)

God created us human beings in an intimate, integral relationship with nature. How may we "progress" in ways which might reinforce rather than weaken the relationship?

> God, who made the world and everything in it, is Lord of heaven and earth, and does not live in temples made by men. Nor does he need anything that [we] can supply by working for him, since it is he himself who gives life and breath and everything else to [everyone]. (Acts 17:24-25, TEV; see verses 24-31)

Concerning Justice

In spite of the fact that the Pacific does not know grinding poverty, the global and the biblical experience insist that we deal with wrong economic and power relationships. The Exodus story reveals God as one who especially loves and cares for the poor and delivers them

out of their poverty and oppression (Exodus 3:7-10). God liberates them in order that they may be God's people, serving God with their whole heart and life (Exodus 6:5-7; Deuteronomy 26:5-8; 1 Samuel 2:2-8; Proverbs 14:31, 19:17).

That liberation became a basis by which they were to live as they became a nation. They were to recognize that the poor have rights, and that they are not simply the objects of charity or voluntary benevolence of the rich but rather are to be protected by law from exploitation by the rich (Exodus 22:25-27; Leviticus 19:9-10, 13-15, 25:35-38; Deuteronomy 24:17-22).

The prophets announced God's judgment because justice had been perverted and the rights of the poor denied. They proclaimed the hope of a future kingdom where peace, righteousness and justice would abound in a new, redeemed society (Isaiah 11:15, 9:6-7, 61:1-2; Jeremiah 23:5-6; Ezekiel 34:17-24).

The psalmists looked to a future in which justice for the poor would prevail, through the coming of the One who would establish justice (Psalms 72:12-14, 140:12, 146).

Jesus' coming was seen as the fulfillment of the hope proclaimed by the prophets for one who would "put down the mighty from their thrones, and exalt those of low degree, ... fill the hungry with good things, and send the rich away empty." (Adapted from Luke 1:52-53)

Unwelcome testing of nuclear weapons, the dumping of radioactive wastes, and all other forms of continued colonization of the Pacific represent injustice: unjust relationships between nations, between regions, between generations.

> Some of you are not satisfied with eating the best grass; you even trample down what you don't eat! You drink the clear water and muddy what you don't drink! My other sheep have to eat the grass you trample down and drink the water you muddy. (Ezekiel 34:18-19, TEV)

> What he requires of us is this: to do what is just, to show constant love, and to live in humble fellowship with our God. (Micah 6:8, TEV)

How do we confront the whole reality of sin? Not only the arrogance, greed and broken relationships of individuals, but also the institutional sin of nations, groups, companies, which puts the narrow national or corporate self-interest ahead of all other considerations. How shall we as a Pacific community responsibly relate to such a frustrating, difficult, but critically important task?

> For we are not fighting against human beings but against the wicked spiritual forces in the heavenly world, the rulers, authorities, and cosmic powers of this dark age. (Ephesians 6:12, TEV)

> No one is holy like the Lord; there is none like him, no protector like our God. Stop your loud boasting; silence your proud words. For the Lord is a God who knows, and he judges all that people do. The bows of strong soldiers are broken, but the weak grow strong. The people who once were well fed now hire themselves out to get food, but the hungry are hungry no more. The childless wife has borne seven children, but the mother of many is left with none. The Lord kills and restores to life; he sends people to the world of the dead and brings them back again. He makes some men poor and others rich; he humbles some and makes others great. He lifts the poor from the dust and raises the needy from their misery. He makes them companions of princes and puts them in places of honor. The foundations of the earth belong to the Lord; on them he has built the world. (1 Samuel 2:2-8, TEV)

> If you oppress poor people, you insult the God who made them; but kindness shown to the poor is an act of worship. (Proverbs 14:31, TEV)

> The kind of fasting I want is this: Remove the chains of oppression and the yoke of injustice, and let the oppressed go free. Share your food with the hungry and open your homes to the homeless poor. Give clothes to those who have nothing to wear, and do not refuse to help your own relatives. Then my favor will shine on you like the morning sun, and your wounds will be quickly healed. I will always be with you to save you; my presence will protect you on every side. (Isaiah 58:6-8, TEV)

> And now, you rich people, listen to me! Weep and wail over the miseries that are coming upon you! Your riches have rotted away, and your clothes have been eaten by moths. Your gold and silver are covered with rust, and this rust will be a witness against you.... (James 5:1-3a, TEV)

Concerning Peacemaking

Upon what are we depending for our security? How can we in the Pacific help to challenge humankind in its brokenness to take risks for peace? Considering the realities of the 1980s and beyond, what is "good thinking" regarding reconciliation, peace, security?

Those who go to Egypt for help are doomed! They are relying on Egypt's vast military strength—horses, chariots, and soldiers. But they do not rely on the Lord, the holy God of Israel, or ask him for help. He knows what he is doing! He sends disaster. He carries out his threats to punish evil men and those who protect them. The Egyptians are not gods—they are only human. Their horses are not supernatural. When the Lord acts, the strong nation will crumble, and the weak nation it helped will fall. Both of them will be destroyed. (Isaiah 31:1-3, TEV; see whole chapter)

How may we contribute to dialogue leading toward new peace dynamics in the world, toward a reduction of the fear and mistrust which has the world locked into a terrible armaments and energy race?

I urge you, then—I who am a prisoner because I serve the Lord: live a life that measures up to the standard God set when he called you. Be always humble, gentle, and patient. Show your love by being tolerant with one another. Do your best to preserve the unity which the Spirit gives by means of the peace that binds you together. (Ephesians 4:1-3, TEV)

And look out for one another's interests, not just for your own. The attitude you should have is the one that Christ Jesus had: He always had the nature of God, but he did not think that by force he should try to become equal with God. Instead of this, of his own free will he gave up all he had, and took the nature of a servant. He became like man and appeared in human likeness. He was humble and walked the path of obedience all the way to death —his death on the cross. (Philippians 2:4-8, TEV)

Come and see what the Lord has done. See what amazing things he has done on earth. He stops wars all over the world; he breaks bows, destroys spears, and sets shields on fire. "Stop fighting," he says, "and know that I am God, supreme among the nations, supreme over the world." (Psalm 46:8-10, TEV; see whole of Psalm 46)

But if you act like wild animals, hurting and harming each other, then watch out, or you will completely destroy one another. (Galatians 5:15, TEV; see Galatians 5:13-15)

"Put your sword back in its place," Jesus said to him. "All who take the sword will die by the sword." (Matthew 26:52, TEV)

All this is done by God, who through Christ changed us from enemies into his friends and gave us the task of making others his friends also. Our message is that God was making all mankind his friends through Christ. (2 Corinthians 5:18-19a, TEV)

Pacific Tingting

Not the thoughts of Chairman Mao
Not the genius animality of Stalin
Not the evil calculation of Marx's dialectics
Not the piousness of soft clericals
Not the rationalization of scientists
and philosophers of immorality
Not the greed of capitalist inhumanity
Not the sentimentality of detente
Neither the nihilism of intellectuals
Nor the brutality of fascism
But the dynamism of quietness
In the hearts of our people
Checking each fault
Calming each fear
Speaking as the ocean breeze at sunset
Of shedding greed
Of shedding hate
New men, new women
Our latent might
Pacific Free!
Pacific Peace!

Kumalau Tawali

First published in *Mana*; reprinted with thanks to *Pacific Islands Monthly*.

PART TWO:

MEET THE PACIFIC PEOPLES

Editor's Note: The Reverend Daniel Mastapha, a Fijian of Indian descent, has risen in leadership within the Methodist Church. Recently he served as moderator, the first Fijian of Indian descent to do so.

You have already met Lorine Tevi, a Fijian who has been a high school teacher and principal of Davuilevu Lay Training Center for school dropouts. She is an active member of the Methodist Church of Fiji with an intense commitment to ecumenical solidarity among Pacific Island peoples. In 1976, Tevi was appointed general secretary of the Pacific Conference of Churches, serving through the 1981 Fourth Assembly. She is now on the education staff of the World Council of Churches in Geneva.

Dr. Gabriel Gris is from Papua New Guinea. Before his appointment to the South Pacific Bureau for Economic Cooperation, he had a distinguished career in government and education in Papua New Guinea, capped by his tenure as chancellor of the University of Papua New Guinea. He is also a church leader of distinction.

Albert Leomala is from Vanuatu, where he was among the first university graduates to return to Vanuatu to teach in the early 1970s. Leomala wrote the poem included here as a student during the early years of the movement for self-government and independence.

B. David Williams, Jr.

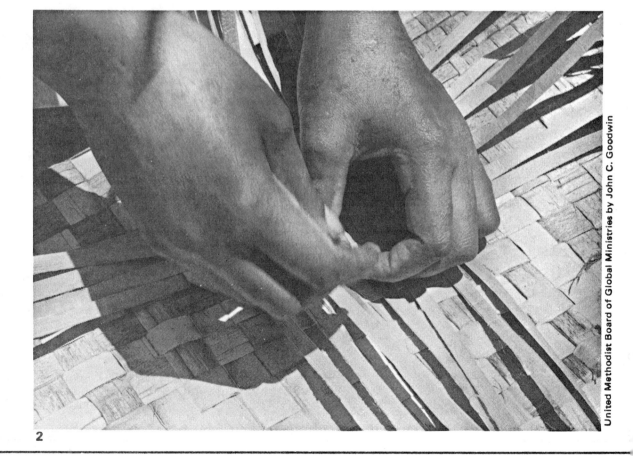

United Methodist Board of Global Ministries by John C. Goodwin

1. *Delegates to the PCC's Fourth Assembly pictured here represent the Solomon Islands, Vanuatu, Australia, Cook Islands, Tonga, Western Samoa, Fiji and New Zealand.*

2. *Skilled hands perform the arts and crafts that are integral to the culture and economy of the Pacific.*

3

4

United Methodist Board of Global Ministries by John C. Goodwin

5

B. David Williams, Jr.

3. *A village scene in the highlands near Wau, Papua New Guinea.*

4. *Many faces make up the countenance of a multicultural society.*

5. *Pasteur Jacques Ajapuhnya, president of the Evangelical Church of New Caledonia, speaking at the PCC's Fourth Assembly; those with earphones are hearing a translation of the French-speaking leader's words.*

LIFE IN A MULTICULTURAL SOCIETY

Daniel Mastapha

The Pacific is the largest ocean in the world. There are more islands in the Pacific than there are in all the other oceans in the world. The Pacific covers one-third of the earth. On the west are the continents of Asia and Australia, on the east the continents of North and South America, and on the south the snow- and ice-covered Antarctic.

People and Space in the Fourth World

The small groups of islands scattered throughout the massive Pacific can be divided into three groups.

The first group is Polynesia, which means "many islands." Situated mainly in the Eastern Pacific, Polynesia includes such islands as Tonga, Samoa, Maori, French Polynesia and Hawaii. The Polynesian peoples are big in stature and have brown skin.

The second group is Melanesia, meaning "dark islands"; it takes its name from the fact that the Melanesians have dark brown skin. These are mainly Western Pacific islands, and include the Solomons, Vanuatu and Papua New Guinea. Fiji is between Polynesia and Melanesia.

The third group is Micronesia, meaning "small islands," and consists largely of very small coral islands and atolls, mainly in the Northern Pacific, such as Kiribati, Tuvalu, Nauru, and the Carolines and Marianas. The people also have brown skins, but are not as dark as the Melanesians.

With the exception of Australia, New Zealand, Papua New Guinea and Fiji, the population of the many different island groups in the Pacific is only in the thousands.

Geographically, many of these island groups are separated by vast reaches of ocean, thus isolated from one another and from the rest of the world. The situation in recent years has improved considerably. Regular communication continues to improve in many island groups with frequent air and sea services to the outside world and within the groups. In spite of improved communication and travel, the problem of distance is still there.

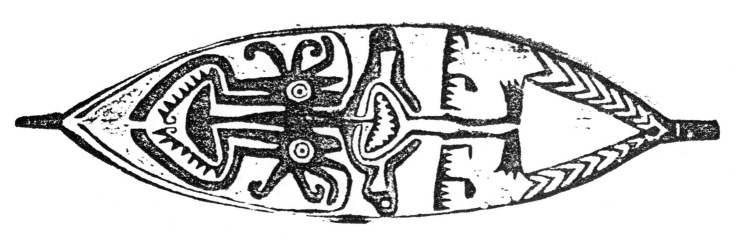

Even within a group, islands can be hundreds of miles away from each other. Rotuma is 300 miles away from the rest of Fiji, and travel in the Pacific is very expensive, particularly for a people who live at the subsistence level in an area where air and sea fares and freight charges are the most expensive in the world. So the experience of isolation and the sense of loneliness and difficult communication are still real here.

The Pacific Islands are a world in themselves — the area has been called the Fourth World. People of each island group differ from one another in stature, skin color, language, dress, eating habits, and social and cultural customs. There are even many differences among people within a particular group of islands. The Pacific is a world of its own — a unique world. Many features in Pacific culture and customs are not found anywhere else. Here is a world of diversities and similarities.

Some Similarities in Culture

Amid the many kinds of diversity among the Pacific people, we cannot overlook the many features in which the Island people are similar to one another.

The people of Polynesia and Melanesia and some of the Micronesians generally live in villages. Generally, houses are grouped together around the chief's house. The people live together like one large extended family and practice communal village life. In many cases, the roots of the people are from the same one or two clans.

While individual families are self-contained and live separately, overall there is a communal living and sharing. Much of the work in the village is done together. Often women go out in a team for fishing or shelling. There is a common loyalty, respect and obedience to the chief or the elder of the village. There is respect for the older people and for the village system. The church in the village is the most important building, respected by all, and all church activities are supported by all. All the people come together and pool their resources for any special function.

The friendliness and happy, laughing mood of the Islanders are universally known and admired. One sees very few long faces among Island people. Island people have few resources and little personal property, yet outsiders are continually amazed by their generous hospital-ity. For a visitor, a stranger or an outsider, whoever he may be, they will prepare the best food available — and plenty of it. If you arrive at mealtime, there is no problem; you are invited to join in and share with others whatever is there. Root crops and seafood are always part of the meal. Every visitor is given some gifts before leaving.

Some of these Pacific Islands are volcanic, hilly, rocky, and all are surrounded by salty water. Natural resources are very limited or nonexistent — the greatest resource in the islands is people. They have no great wealth from a Western point of view, yet their wealth is in their hearts. Their respect for others, their generosity, their hospitality and friendliness are some of the great qualities of Island people.

Winds of Change

With better and faster communication, with modern technology and new roads, the Pacific Islands are facing many rapid and radical changes. Coupled with these is the influx of the Western way of life. All these factors are affecting the culture and way of life of the Island people. Some of the changes are very rapid, and the people are not able to adjust themselves or assimilate them. Tourism is having a great effect on thinking, dressing and in other ways. Western kinds of education are having a very strong influence on the Island people. Some of these changes are good, but others are not so good.

Liquor has become the number one social problem in many of the Islands, especially Fiji, Tonga, Samoa and Papua New Guinea. Gambling is becoming common and many people want to live by luck and chance instead of hard work. Nearly all Pacific Islands are Christian and Sunday is set aside traditionally as a day of worship and rest, but this observance is breaking down very fast. Many tourist ships call in at the Islands on Sundays.

Because of limited resources, new jobs are few and unemployment is becoming a serious problem in many islands. As a result, there is mass migration from Tonga, Samoa, the Cook Islands and Niue to Australia, New Zealand, Hawaii and the mainland United States. With new roads and better communication, the drift to towns and cities is increasing, causing new problems. Many young people are unemployed and displaced, turning to crime, hooliganism and drinking. The transition from

subsistence living to a money economy, plus inflation, is making life burdensome and strenuous for many island people.

The village extended family system is changing to nuclear family life. The breakdown of marriage and disintegration of family life are growing into serious problems. The process of urbanization, development of land, new roads, electrification and new water systems make life more easy and comfortable but at the same time bring new problems and a more complicated life.

These changes are having great effects on the multicultural society of the Pacific Islands. The changes are also affecting the churches.

A Multicultural Society

The Pacific Islands are a meeting place for many cultures from throughout the world. The different Island groups each have their own culture. In some, imported cultures exist alongside the indigenous culture. Here are some brief examples.

In Vanuatu and New Caledonia, the indigenous Island culture exists alongside European culture. Fiji is a meeting place of three dominant cultures: the Pacific culture, Western culture, and Asiatic Indian or Chinese cultures. In Fiji, the Rotuman and the Banaban island customs also exist, as well as other Pacific Island cultures like those of the Tongans, Samoans and Solomon Islanders.

New Zealand is becoming very much a multicultural society. There are the western Pakeha (Maori word for white person), the Polynesian culture of the Maoris, the Samoans, Niuans, Cook Islanders and Tongans. All these Island groups have significant communities in New Zealand, and their different cultures are enriching one another's way of life.

There are Chinese in Nauru and Japanese in Micronesia, having great effect on the life of the indigenous people. Then there is movement of people from one Island group to another. There are many people from Tuvalu and Kiribati in Nauru.

The Pacific is rightly called a multicultural society, where different cultures exist alongside one another, interacting and enriching one another.

The traditional dance is common to all Island groups. This dance can be very vigorous and colorful, and it can also be quiet and graceful. Its rhythm, action and singing in unison can be very exciting. The dances differ from one Island group to another.

In Polynesia the traditional way of preparing a feast uses an underground oven. This method of cooking always produces tasty and appetizing food. While Fijians would roast a pig in an earth oven, Tongans use an open fire. Islanders are good sailors and great fishermen. Fish and other seafood are part of a normal meal.

Kava, a mildly intoxicant plant, is used in many Islands for ceremonial purposes in a variety of ways, but in many Islands it has become a common social drink. In Fiji, excessive kava drinking is affecting the lives of some, interfering with work.

The coconut is the national tree of the Island people. Its peculiar shape and majestic height add to the beauty of the tropical islands, and it lends itself to a wide variety of uses. Dry nuts are used for cooking and for oil, green ones for drinking and eating, leaves for weaving baskets and thatching roofs and trunks for building posts.

Fijians use tabua (whale's teeth) for many traditional ceremonies. This is unique, not only in the Pacific, but in the world.

Mats are made out of dried needle-shaped leaves. Mats in different shapes and sizes and of differing weaves are common in all the Islands. They are used for bedding, floor covering and gifts. Tapa or masi is made out of beaten bark from special trees and is common in Tonga, Samoa and Fiji. Tapa is very popular with tourists. It is used for table mats, wall decoration, bedding and gifts for marriages and funerals.

The Pacific Islands are mostly tropical. People normally dress lightly, but they are well-dressed. Most men wear a sulu or lavalava (a formal men's skirt, originally introduced by Protestant missionaries, also called the rami or pareu or laplap; a relaxed version in gay floral print is worn informally, especially at home). The Island women are traditionally nicely dressed, with long dress and sulu right down to the ground. Indian women in Fiji wear their traditional saris.

Christianity and Culture

Christianity came to the Islands during the last century. This one single force changed much of the way of life of the Island people. Christianity in the Pacific has transformed much of the culture, but the church remains

very much in its Western form and garb. Its patterns of preaching and singing, and its forms of worship, are Western. In some cases, the missionaries transplanted the cultural values of their own nations. This gave the people the impression that Western culture was superior to their own culture. The missionaries duplicated the denominational patterns with which they were affiliated. This Christian competition has confused many Island Christians also. Today the influx of Christian sects into the Islands is still confusing. The missionaries brought the seed of the gospel in a pot and planted it with the pot around it instead of planting the seed in the indigenous Island soil.

However, while the Christian faith is still in Western garb, it has transformed the culture of the people, and in many cases it has preserved what is good and meaningful to the people. Christianity is the way of life of the Island people. While many are sincere, practicing Christians, there is a problem of nominalism—to some it is simply a Sunday religion. However, today there emerges new meaning and understanding of the Christian faith. There are signs of renewal and revival among Island Christians. There is also a real resurgence of Pacific culture in the Islands, with new interest in reviving and practicing Island ways.

The Pacific, the Fourth World, is the home of a family of people who are different from one another in a variety of ways yet who feel they belong together in their faith, aspirations and struggle to better themselves and future generations. They continue to accept changes in the light of their Christian faith. The Pacific, a multicultural society, is the home of some of the finest Christians in the world.

United Methodist Board of Global Ministries by John C. Goodwin

Traditional Fijian "Make Make" dancers.

THE PACIFIC CONFERENCE OF CHURCHES
Lorine Tevi

Every Pacific Island person and even people from overseas who have worked in, lived in or visited the Pacific, know that the Christian church has a very strong and influential role in the Pacific communities. The church is the strong, uniting force in our environment. Now, as the spirit of regionalism and Pacific cooperation and solidarity is becoming stronger, we are thankful to God and to the pioneers of the Pacific Conference of Churches for the inspiration and initiative taken to establish the Pacific Conference of Churches.

The Birth of the Pacific Conference of Churches

History has proved that when any major event takes place, it originates from one mind, is shared with others for interaction and recreation, and if successful, comes to reality. Thus was the beginning of the Pacific Conference of Churches. Toward the end of World War II, some young ministers from the Pacific islands were stranded in Australia and attended church conferences held in that country. When they met together they realized the need for the Pacific people to work together, and they became convinced that the formation of a regional Christian organization would help strengthen their witness and unity in Jesus Christ. Two of these young leaders were the Rev. Setareki Tuilovoni of Fiji and Dr. Sione Amanaki Havea of Tonga, well-known Christians who are still serving in the Pacific today.

After the war there were already movements of Christian missionaries from the South Pacific to Papua New Guinea, Solomon Islands and the New Hebrides. As the ministers traveled to the different islands, they would stop for a couple of days to preach and share stories and bring greetings from their churches to the congregations present. In the early 1950s, Christian youth organizations were established and this led to the building of a regional youth convention in the second half of that decade, bringing Tongans, Fijians and Samoans together as delegates. They spent one week in Bible study, seminars, sports and worship in their youth convention. Visiting other islands before or after the youth convention added to their understanding and appreciation of Pacific islands' values.

Besides the interaction with the church youth, young people who came to the Fiji Medical School, the Nursing School and other schools in Suva and Fiji from many other islands in the Pacific developed closer relationships and feelings of regional solidarity. All these things helped Pacific islanders to know one another better. Intermarriages took place that also strengthened these bonds.

Even though the idea of a regional organization was already in the minds of some of the indigenous Pacific church leaders, it was the London Missionary Society which initiated the move, through correspondence with the churches and missions in the Pacific area. In February 1959, the International Missionary Council was invited by the churches and missions to organize a conference of churches and missions operating in the Pacific area. The churches wanted a small study conference in the Pacific way that would allow ample time for informal conversation, so that representatives could hear about one another's faith, life and work.

The Pacific churches and missionary agencies held the

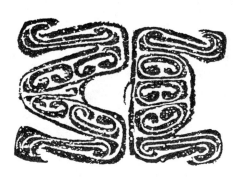

first meeting at Malua Theological College in Western Samoa in 1961. In preparation for this conference, the participating churches and missions were invited to discuss the theme of the conference in their regular church services. The letter to the Galatians was to be the basis of Bible study, and churches were asked to pray for the conference and give it wide publicity.

When the church leaders and members met, the needs of the Pacific churches were discussed. It was felt necessary to upgrade theological training for ministers and church workers. Up to the time of the meeting, most of those who continued their ministerial formation beyond local theological colleges went to Australia, New Zealand, England, the United States and India. The participants were convinced that a regional ecumenical college was what was needed to serve the majority and to give relevant theological education programs.

Another major need expressed was the preparation of a relevant Sunday school syllabus and appropriate materials. Up to 1961, most of the churches were translating materials from overseas churches.

The need for an interchurch organization led to the formation of the Pacific Conference of Churches. The meeting decided to appoint a continuation committee to act on some of the resolutions and to work on the preparation of the constitution. For five years the continuation committee worked hard, trying to implement the resolutions of the conference.

The resolution recommending a central theological college was taken up, and a planning group was formed. The group met in Suva, Fiji, and gathered the interest and support not only of Pacific churches, but of overseas cooperating churches and the Theological Education Fund (of the World Council of Churches). By 1965 new buildings were under construction, and in 1966 the first students were in residence at the Pacific Theological College in Suva.

At Colo-i-Suva, in Fiji, coeditors had been working on another important united project. After a curriculum consultation and writers' workshop in 1963, work began on the preparation of Christian Education material for the Pacific. The now well-known Pacific Islands Christian Education Curriculum (PICEC) was under way. Educational material from people all over the Pacific was received, edited and prepared for the Christian Educa-

tion program. This material was relevant to the life and needs of Pacific people.

At the suggestion of the continuation committee, delegates from different churches and territories exchanged visits. At its meetings, the committee itself was wrestling with a constitution which would give a form to all this cooperation and development. The more we got to know each other, the more we recognized how much we had in common and how many of our difficulties were mutual. The drift by rural people to the towns and cities, industrialization, lack of housing in the towns, tourism and the challenges to our Christian faith were all problems we shared. It was important for us to seek each other's help in facing them. The day had certainly come when the churches of the South Pacific needed to establish firm links.

In 1966, at Lifou in the Loyalty Islands of New Caledonia, the Pacific churches and mission boards met to constitute the Pacific Conference of churches at its first Assembly. This was a great occasion, when representatives from the many churches in the region came with the responses confirming the need for such a regional organization. The second Assembly was held in Davuilevu, Fiji, in 1971, the third in Port Moresby, Papua New Guinea, in 1976, and the fourth is planned for Tonga in 1981.

Since its constitution, the PCC endeavors to be true to its basis as "a fellowship of churches which confess the Lord Jesus Christ as God and Savior according to the Scriptures and therefore seek to fulfill together their common calling to the glory of the one God, Father, Son, and Holy Spirit." The main function of the PCC is to support local churches so that they can carry out their ministries and to share at the regional level experiences and challenges common to all as they seek to witness to the Lord Jesus Christ.

Major Programs of the Pacific Conference of Churches

As the services of the PCC continued to develop, different programs also took shape. PICEC later became the Christian Education Programme of the PCC. The publishing arm became Lotu Pasifika Productions. A later development was Chriscom, a Christian Education

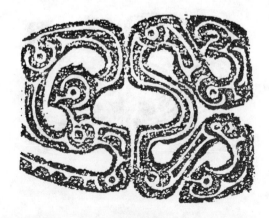

and Communication Programme (CEAC) of the PCC. At present, Christian Education is the program dealing with lay training, children's work, group work, youth work, Bible study, etc., while the communication program deals with radio work and other communication media. In addition, there are the Family Life Programme and the Church and Society Programme. Two new programs which have been formed since the third Assembly are the Pacific Churches Research Centre based in Vila, Vanuatu, and the Chaplaincy to the University of the South Pacific.

The Family Life Programme, presently based in Papua New Guinea, aims at promoting study of various aspects of family life, a leadership training program, marriage enrichment, sex education, counseling and production of appropriate literature. The Church and Society Programme deals with matters concerning economics, nuclear issues, politics, colonialism and integral human development. In general, it assists the churches to understand their mission as transformers of the world according to the values of the Kingdom of God.

This is the third year in which the PCC offers the service of a chaplain to the University of the South Pacific. Because the University prepares regional leaders, the churches felt that it was important to attend to their spiritual needs and religious development. During the past two years, the University chaplain has spent most of his time in pastoral care and counseling of students and staff.

The newest part of the PCC organization is the Pacific Churches Research Centre. The Centre was established as a response to a need felt by the church to encourage Pacific people to study and research their own religion, history, culture and social organization. Since its establishment in late 1978, the Centre has proved very successful, and the PCC sees it as an important serving arm of the organization.

Issues for Today

In addition to the above program, there are certain issues which the PCC is working on and wishes to emphasize.

Spiritual Renewal and Deepening of the Faith. The ministry of the church is always one of mission and service, especially where the evangelical and serving role of the Christian faith is expressed. With the rapid changes occurring in the Pacific region, Christians are seeking the reality of a loving and caring God. The problems and issues confronting us daily help us to raise important theological questions regarding the Christian faith. It is only when beliefs are well-founded, with a strong theological and biblical basis for action, that people can be inspired to take the initiative to involve themselves creatively in the community and to give witness to these beliefs.

Integral Human Development. For the PCC, the 1970s were a decade of meetings, seminars and consultations in the area of development. Ten such meetings have been held since 1970. The Rev. Sitiveni Ratuvili, a former PCC staff member, stated in his book, *Spiritual Bases for Rural Development*:

> Development cannot be developed unless it is integral. That is, it must promote the good of every man and the whole man. Man is not made up of different compartments. He has been blessed with feelings, aspirations, hope and a mind to think, all of which comprise an entity. One cannot separate one from the whole. If we have tried to help a person to participate in a project which could fill his pocket, then we must also prepare him in the area of stewardship. Integral human development also assumes that man is inseparable from the society to which he belongs and from which he derives his security and identity. If we are sincere in our efforts to help people grow, then we must also look at the social conditions in which they live.

With the above philosophy and modest asking of integral human development, the PCC cannot help but become involved in every aspect of the life of the people in the Pacific. We cannot separate or compartmentalize our services, because we believe and accept that God creates the whole person.

Pacific Identity and Solidarity. For ecumenical work in the region and for regional cooperation, it is of vital importance that the Pacific churches clearly identify who they are. As people of the region meet to share their faith, concerns, traditions and aspirations in an atmosphere of Christian love and fellowship and as they move with the leadership of the Holy Spirit, an authentic

identity could evolve that would bring a new sense of commitment to cooperation and solidarity. It is the churches who will have to lay the foundation of the Pacific identity and solidarity.

Theological Education and Reshaping of Educational Ministries. The PCC believes that if the mission and service of the churches is to be effective, the formation and preparation of the ministers and the laity needs to be looked at seriously. In education for ministry, the emphasis should be on horizontal rather than hierarchical relationships. Preparing ministers and leaders able to interact with the communities compels the churches to take the community development approach to educational ministries.

Independence Movements. In 1976, the PCC Assembly stated in relation to the New Hebrides:

> We, the Pacific Conference of Churches, in the name of justice and Human Rights, condemn the manner in which the British and French Governments have unduly maintained their political domination over the New Hebrides, urge Britain and France to take immediate constructive steps toward building up political unity and achievement of independence for the New Hebrides, and require the member churches and the ecumenical organizations represented here to bring the need of the New Hebrides to the attention of their respective governments.

Since the Assembly, the struggle in the New Hebrides has led to the achievement of the country's independence on July 31, 1980. The country's new name is Vanuatu.

The situation in Vanuatu and New Caledonia are two examples of what is happening now and what will continue to happen in the 1980s regarding countries which are still under the control of colonial powers. The solidarity and unity of the Pacific peoples can never be fully achieved as long as there are countries in the Pacific that are still being dominated by foreign powers.

Nuclear-Free Pacific. The PCC stand is clear: it condemns the testing of nuclear bombs in the Pacific. It condemns the dumping of nuclear waste in the Pacific and the movement of nuclear weapon ships through Pacific waters. At present, in spite of protests from the people and governments of the Pacific regarding nuclear policies, the colonial powers do not listen to our protests.

"We are bitterly opposed to our people, environment, and future generations being subjected to the danger and irreversible damage of radioactive contamination."

The church's stand on nuclear matters is based on the principles:

1. Human life is God's gift. It must be respected as such.
2. Every person has a right to live. Nuclear radiation endangers this right.
3. Every person has a right to have peace. The presence of nuclear weapons creates fear, not peace.
4. Inventions should be encouraged to help people to live with dignity and freedom but not to enslave them.

Participation of Women and Youth. Women and youth in the changing Pacific are now asserting their rights to be equal partners with men. They need to be set free from the psychological disadvantage in which tradition and society have placed them. They need to be empowered to participate freely in decision-making at all levels in the community.

Transnational Corporations. As in other developing countries, transnational corporations (TNCs) are also making an impact in the Pacific region. The executive committee of the PCC has requested the Church and Society Programme to make a serious study of this subject, particularly with regard to the impact of TNCs upon Pacific values and upon Pacific political decisions.

Tourism. The attraction of the South Sea Islands for tourism has brought both advantages and disadvantages. The negative effects cannot be evaded. Tourism is in the Pacific and it is here to stay. The church's role is to deal creatively with it. The churches are just beginning to look critically at the situation. The PCC also sees that in order to try to avoid the problems that tourism brings, there has to be partnership in mission between both the sending and the hosting countries.

Aid and Development. The Pacific countries are receiving enormous amounts of money for development through governments as well as nongovernmental organizations. Concern has been expressed about the disadvantages as well as the advantages of this aid. It is the objective of the PCC to support the churches and the countries in the region in their efforts to determine what they believe will be best for their countries, without

being dominated or tied down by conditions set by the donor agencies. A more serious question is the motivation for giving such large amounts of aid over a long period to countries in the region. There is no doubt that the Pacific will be the center of the struggle for power during the next decade. How can the majority of the Pacific people be equipped to help meet the 1980s and 1990s? An important role of the church will be to effectively share its philosophy of integral human development.

Some Special Priorities

In an endeavor to help cope with these and other issues in the region, the PCC executive committee has decided that the PCC approach toward wholeness in mission must give special attention and focus to these priorities:

> The biblical and theological basis for the renewal of the church and for integral human development. The biblical and theological basis for the renewal of society, particularly in marriage and in family structure, the creative involvement and participation of children, youth and women.

These priorities have been chosen with the conviction that it is the calling of the church today to concentrate on renewing and deepening its life through biblical and theological reflection, in order to activate authentically its wholeness in mission.

In May of 1981 the PCC will hold its fourth Assembly in Tonga. Member churches are discussing the issues before they come to the Assembly so that they can be involved with the biblical and theological reflections before and during the meeting. Church leaders and different groups have been meeting to discover just what is happening now and what will develop in the Pacific during the next decade and in following years.

If the churches are to be Christ's church today, they must play their prophetic and servicing role in giving inspiration, hope and joy to the people's life. This role can only be achieved when church leaders and members become aware of the reality and the truth of what is happening. With biblical and theological reflection as the basis for action, the PCC believes that God will call the Pacific people to create a society where God's King-

dom can be more of a reality.

This is not going to be easy because it may mean doing away with some of the things which have been and are still seen as essentials of the churches. The churches in the Pacific will have to find and experience their own crosses and their own calvary. It was only when Christ decided to carry the calvary cross that his mission became more authentic and successful.

Conclusion

There is no other regional organization that has such a good structural network as the Pacific Conference of Churches. As I mentioned earlier, the churches in each country have a strong influence on Pacific communities. The majority of the people in the Pacific still have faith in the churches and hold them in high regard. I am convinced that when the two priorities for special attention are activated in the different churches throughout the region, people will become more aware of what is actually happening. When they become more aware of the truth, with the guidance of the Holy Spirit they will move to do God's will, to effect God's Kingdom more and more in their home, community, nations and the region.

As the majority of Pacific people become more aware of their situation, they will also become more aware of the rest of the world and how other countries affect them and vice versa. In trying to see the wholeness of God's mission in the Pacific region, we are involved in serving God's mission in the whole world. The Pacific has a great deal to contribute to the rest of the world and vice versa. The challenge now is to know how to come to grips with this Pacific reality and its uniqueness before it can be shared. The vision of the PCC is to work with the member churches in the region and to help them rediscover their Pacific identity, to uphold Pacific solidarity in the light of the gospel and to make the pilgrimage that God makes with God's people.

A REGIONAL OVERVIEW

Gabriel Gris

The South Pacific Forum and the South Pacific Bureau for Economic Cooperation (SPEC) are the two most significant agencies for regional cooperation among those Pacific Island countries that have achieved either independence or self-government in the last twenty years.

The Islands of the South Pacific

Western Samoa led the South Pacific in attaining political independence on January 1, 1962. The Cook Islands in 1965 attained the status of a self-governing state in free association with New Zealand. On January 31, 1968, Nauru became an independent republic. It was followed by Fiji, which became independent on October 10, 1970. Niue achieved the same status in relation to New Zealand as the Cook Islands on October 19, 1974. Papua New Guinea gained her independence from Australia on September 16, 1975. In July and October of 1978, Solomon Islands and Tuvalu respectively gained their independence from the United Kingdom (Great Britain). The Republic of Kiribati attained full nationhood on July 12, 1979. The New Hebrides celebrated her independence on July 30, 1980, and took the name of Vanuatu, while the Federated States of Micronesia was expected to be independent in 1981. Although Tonga never came directly under any colonial rule, she formalized her status as an independent Kingdom on June 4, 1970.

Land areas range from Papua New Guinea's 462,243 square kilometers, with its mountains, major rivers, jungle, highlands and lowlands, to the small coral atolls of Tuvalu. Great distances separate Pacific Island countries from one another and from the rest of the world. For example, the Cook Islands, where the total land area is 240 square kilometers, is made up of 15 islands spread over some 1,830,000 square kilometers of ocean. The nearest markets, Australia and New Zealand, are over 3,000 and 1,760 kilometers respectively from Fiji.

The population of the South Pacific region is about 4.7 million with an average annual rate of increase of 2.6 percent. Papua New Guinea, with a population of nearly 3 million, is by far the largest, followed by Fiji, with a population close to 600,000. Four countries—Solomon Islands, Western Samoa, Vanuatu, and Tonga—have populations ranging from just under 100,000 to above 200,000. Kiribati has a population of 54,000 and the Cook Islands 19,000. Smaller still are Tuvalu with 7,400, Nauru with 7,000 and Niue with 3,500.

Most of the region's island economies are based on agriculture, and future development in this area will continue to be of importance. The future also holds hope for the region in the exploitation of its living marine and seabed resources. Development aspirations of the region will continue to rely on external finance for quite some time.

Origins of Regional Cooperation

The "discovery" of the region by various navigators during the mid-eighteenth century opened it up to missionaries, anthropologists, planters, traders and colo-

nists. These new settlers to the Pacific brought with them a new way of life based on European values and goals. The settlements which they established were far removed from the commercial centers of the world. Survival of the new settlers and protection of their property necessitated certain security measures. Acquisition of territories was a major preoccupation. Later, perpetuation of certain influences became the basis for cooperation among the island administrations.

World War II had a dramatic impact on the South Pacific region and it brought to the attention of the Western powers and especially of Australia and New Zealand the strategic importance of the South Pacific region. These western countries with interests in the South Pacific became concerned not only with the defense of the region but also the "economic and social welfare of the natives." To this end, the colonial powers in the Pacific—the United States, the United Kingdom, France, the Netherlands, Australia and New Zealand—signed the Canberra Agreement which established the South Pacific Commission (SPC) in January 1947, in Canberra, Australia. (The Netherlands withdrew from SPC in 1962.) This signaled a major step forward by the colonial powers which positively committed themselves to the concept of regional cooperation.

The new organization was charged with promoting the "economic and social welfare and advancement of the peoples of the non-self-governing territories in the South Pacific." Throughout the 1950s and early 1960s, the SPC functioned in accordance with the wishes of the colonial powers who were in complete control of its development activities at the policymaking level. The contributions of the Island representatives to the SPC conferences were subject to further consideration by the metropolitan governments.[1] These arrangements were satisfactory at first, but as some island countries moved rapidly toward independence or self-government, their self-confidence grew and they demanded changes that would lead to a more direct participation by them in decision making.

Concessions were made by the metropolitan governments to the island representatives in allowing them more decision-making opportunities in the activities of SPC. In 1969 the first Islander, Afioga Misimosa of Western Samoa, was appointed to the top executive post of Secretary-General.

The South Pacific Forum Emerges

Although these events contributed to the growth of regional awareness in the South Pacific, the "no politics" rule at SPC Conferences continued to raise the ire of Island leaders. The frustrations experienced through the refusal by certain metropolitan representatives to discuss matters of a "political nature" at SPC conferences forced Island leaders to remove their problems of "mutual concern" to another appropriate setting—the South Pacific Forum.

The South Pacific Forum was conceived to be an informal gathering of South Pacific Island leaders from independent and self-governing countries where they could discuss and exchange views on matters of mutual concern in what was and is known as the "Pacific Way." The first informal meeting of the South Pacific Forum was held in Wellington, New Zealand, in August 1971, and was attended by leaders from Fiji, Nauru, Tonga, Western Samoa and Cook Islands, with Australia and New Zealand as observers. Australia and New Zealand subsequently became full members. The Forum was later joined by Papua New Guinea (1974), Niue (1975), Kiribati (1977), Solomon Islands (1978), Tuvalu (1978) and Vanuatu (1980). The Federated States of Micronesia was given observer status in 1980.

To qualify for membership in the Forum, a country has to be an independent or self-governing country in the South Pacific. If a country is near self-government, there must be some broad indication of when self-governing status is actually to be achieved. Membership requires the endorsement of the Forum, and a prospective full member should have competence to implement all decisions, including political decisions, of the Forum.

Search for Economic Union

The first Forum meeting in 1971 decided on a meeting of trade officials to examine "the possibility of establishing an economic union for the area." The trade officials' meeting recommended a secretariat be established to continue to examine regional trade matters. At the Apia Forum in 1973, an agreement was signed establishing the South Pacific Committee for Economic Cooperation (SPEC), conferring a firm mandate over matters of trade and economic development for the region. The institutional structure provided for SPEC under the agreement establishes an executive body, the Committee, and a permanent Secretariat, the Bureau. The Committee usually consists of senior government officials representing member states and it meets twice a year. The Bureau is charged with implementing the mandate given by the SPEC Agreement and other directives given either by the Forum itself or by the Committee. Since 1975, the Bureau has been charged with carrying out secretarial functions for the Forum also.

---

[1] In the South Pacific understanding, "metropolitan governments" are Great Britain, France and the United States.

PACIFIC NATIONS STATISTICS

PAPUA NEW GUINEA

Area: 463,476 sq.km. Comprises half the main island of New Guinea plus nine main island groups and nine smaller groups—some 200 islands in all. Mainland Papua New Guinea, Manus group, New Britain, New Ireland, Bougainville. **Capital:** Port Moresby. **Population:** 3,168,700 (1980 estimate). **Government:** independent — Governor-General and unicameral parliament. **Economy:** Main industries — agriculture (copra, cocoa, coffee, subsistence crops), mining (copper, gold), manufactures. Main exports: coffee, cocoa, copra, coconut oil, timber, copper ore and concentrates. Markets: Australia, Japan, West Germany, Britain, U.S.A. Main imports: Non-electrical machinery, transport equipment, cereals, meat, metal manufactures, foodstuffs. Main suppliers: Australia, U.S.A., U.K., Singapore.

Churches:

Roman Catholic (31%)	800,000
Evangelical Lutheran	500,000
United Church	380,000
Anglican	150,000
Seventh Day Adventist	77,000
Gudnius Lutheran	60,000
Evangelical Alliance	220,000

Christian total (est.) 2,500,000. Belonging to the Melanesian Council of Churches are the Roman Catholic, Lutheran, United, Anglican and Baptist Churches and the Salvation Army. There are also 11 associate member organizations.

NIUE

Area: 258 sq.km. One island. **Capital:** Alofi. **Population:** 3580 plus about 6000 in N.Z. **Economy:** Main industries: copra, tropic fruit and other agriculture, timber, livestock, handicrafts, lime juice. Main exports: copra, passion-fruit, handicrafts, seeds, honey, limes, lime juice. Main markets: N.Z., U.K., Australia. Main imports: foodstuffs, machinery, transport equipment, manufactures, beverages, tobacco, chemicals, mineral fuels. Main suppliers: N.Z., Japan, Singapore, Fiji, Australia.

Churches:

Niuean Church	2,685
Mormon	358
Roman Catholic	180
Jehovah's Witnesses	Some
Seventh Day Adventist	Some

From Vaughan Hinton, ed., *Tides of Change: Pacific Christians Review Their Problems and Hopes* (Melbourne: Commission for World Mission of the Uniting Church in Australia, 1981). Used by permission.

WESTERN SAMOA

Area: 2,934 sq.km. Two main islands, about 20 smaller islands. Upolu, Savai'i. **Capital:** Apia on Upolu. **Population:** 152,000. **Government:** independent parliamentary democracy. **Economy:** Main industries: agriculture, (copra, cocoa, coffee, subsistence crops, tropical fruit, vegetables), livestock, handicrafts, tourism, fisheries, timber, manufactured foodstuffs, light manufactures). Main exports: copra, cocoa, bananas, foodstuffs. Main markets: N.Z., U.K., U.S., Australia, Canada. Main imports: electrical machinery, transport equipment, food, beverages, manufactures. Main suppliers: U.K., Australia, Japan, Canada.

Churches:

Congregational	75,679
Roman Catholic	33,180
Methodist	23,864
Mormon	12,000
Seventh Day Adventist	2,840
Anglican	426

TONGA

Area: 750 sq.km. Three main island groups with 162 islands. Tongatapu, Eua, Haapai, Vava'u Group, Kotu Group. **Capital:** Nuku'alofa on Tongatapu. **Population:** 92,000. **Government:** independent monarchy. **Economy:** Main industries: agriculture (copra, vegetables, fruit), dessicated coconut, tourism. Main exports: copra, bananas, dessicated coconut. Main imports: food, live animals, manufactures, machinery, transport equipment. Main suppliers: N.Z., Australia, Fiji, U.K., Japan. Main markets: Netherlands, N.Z., Australia.

Churches:

Free Wesleyan	42,687
Roman Catholic	14,414
Free Church of Tonga	12,326
Mormon	8,350
Church of Tonga	8,031
Seventh Day Adventist	1,919
Anglican	904
Assemblies of God	338

VANUATU

Area: 11,800 sq.km. Some 80 islands. Efate, Espiritu Santo, Malekula, Tanna, Pentecost, Ambryn, Banks Group). **Capital:** Vila on Efate Island. **Population:** 113,000 (1980 estimate). **Government:** independent — 39-member elected Assembly with Chief Minister. **Economy:** Main industries: agriculture (bananas, taro, copra, cocoa, meat, dairy products), fish, manganese. Main exports: fresh and canned meat, copra, cocoa, coffee. Markets: France, New Caledonia,

Solomon Islands, Tahiti. Main imports: rice, medical supplies, electrical machinery, cars, metal sheeting. Main suppliers: Australia, N.Z., U.K., France.

Churches:

Presbyterian	45,000
Roman Catholic	18,000
Anglican	16,000
Churches of Christ	3,500
Apostolic	1,000
Seventh Day Adventist	4,000
Free Evangelical Church	1,500

Full members of the Vanuatu Christian Council are the Presbyterian, Roman Catholic, Anglican, Churches of Christ and Apostolic Churches. Observer members are Seventh Day Adventists and Assemblies of God. There are various smaller Christian churches and Jehovah's Witnesses and Bahais.

NEW CALEDONIA

Area: 19,103 sq.km. Main islands New Caledonia, Isle of Pines, Loyalty, Belese, Chesterfield Group, Walpole, Surprise, Huon. **Capital:** Noumea on New Caledonia. **Population:** 137,000 (1980 est.) (Includes 56,500 Melanesians, 53,000 Europeans, 7,000 Polynesians, 10,900 Wallisians. **Government:** overseas territory of France, represented in French Parliament. **Economy:** Main industries: mining (nickel, manganese), tourism, agriculture (coffee, copra, meat and dairying). Main exports: nickel, manganese, coffee, copra. Markets: France, Japan. Main imports: transport equipment, mining machinery, manufactures, medical supplies, foodstuffs, clothing. Suppliers: Australia, France.

Churches:

Eglise Catholique	91,000
Eglise Evangelique	20,370
Eglise Evangelique Libre	8,560
Assemblees de Dieu	680
Eglise Adventiste	650
Mormon	530
Reorganized Church of Jesus Christ of Latter Day Saints	320
Anglican	260
Jehovah's Witnesses	620

Other religions:

Bahai	320
Muslim	4,250

SOLOMON ISLANDS

Area: 28,530 sq.km. Ten large islands or groups, 922 islands in all. Guadalcanal, Santa Isabel, San Christobal, Malaita, New Georgia, Choiseul Kolombangara, Vella Lavella, Kennell. **Capital:** Honiara on Guadalcanal. **Population:** 160,998. **Government:** independent — Governor-General with 38-member elected parliament. **Economy:** Main industries: agriculture (copra, cocoa, rice), timber, cattle, fisheries, palm oil, light manufactures. Main exports: copra, timber, fish. Main markets: Japan, Australia, Germany, U.K., N.Z., Papua New Guinea. Main imports: machinery and transport equipment, manufactures, foodstuffs. Main suppliers: U.K., Japan, Singapore.

Churches:

Anglican	53,500
Roman Catholic	30,590
South Seas Evangelical	27,370
United	17,710
Seventh Day Adventist	16,100
Christian Fellowship	3,500
Jehovah's Witnesses	3,000

Other religions:

Bahai	800

There are small groups of Assemblies of God, Missionary Baptist Church of California and South Pacific Evangelical Fellowship.

FIJI

Area: 18,376 sq.km. Some 320 islands, 105 inhabited. Viti Levu, Vanua Levu, Taveuni, Lau, Kadavu, Lomaiviti Group, Yasawa Group, Rotuma Group. **Capital:** Suva on Viti Levu. **Population:** 612,046. Includes 272,447 Fijians, 306,957 Indians, 3,393 Europeans, 10,721 part-Europeans, 4,633 Chinese, 5,442 other Pacific Islanders, 7,619 Rotumans. **Government:** independent. Governor-General and bi-cameral parliamentary system. **Economy:** Main industries: sugar, tourism, copra, gold, other agriculture, manufacturing. Exports: sugar, gold, coconut products, molasses. Markets: Britain, Australia, N.Z., U.S.A., Canada. Imports: machinery and transport equipment, manufacturing, foodstuffs, mineral fuels. Suppliers: Australia, Japan, U.K., N.Z.

Churches:

Methodist	219,900
Roman Catholic	49,800
Seventh Day Adventist	9,300
Assemblies of God	7,100
Anglican	5,700
Presbyterian	619
Other Christian	7,200

Other religions:

Hindu	234,520
Muslim	45,247

FRENCH POLYNESIA

Area: 4,000 sq.km. More than 400 islands. Society Islands, Windward Islands, Leeward Islands, Marquesas Islands. **Capital:** Papeete on Tahiti. **Population:** 140,000. **Government:** overseas territory of France. **Economy:** Main industries: agriculture (copra, tobacco, vanilla, tropical fruit), tourism, livestock, small boat building, fisheries. Main exports: copra, tobacco, vanilla, canned fish, tropical fruit. Main markets: France, West Germany, Australia. Main imports: canned food, household equipment, manufactures. Main suppliers: France, U.S.A., Australia, N.Z., U.K.

Churches:

Societe des Missions Evangeliques de Paris	70,000
Seventh Day Adventist	2,800
Mormon	8,500
Roman Catholic	46,000

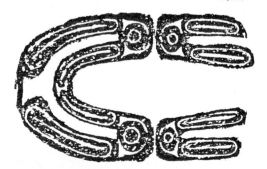

AMERICAN SAMOA

Area: 196 sq.km. Sixty inhabited, 20 small uninhabited islands. Tutuila, Aunuu, Swains, Manu's group. **Capital:** Pago Pago. **Population:** 31,000. **Government:** U.S. unincorporated territory with government and bicameral legislature. **Economy:** Main industries: fish canning, watch manufacturing. Main exports: canned fish, fish meal. Main markets: U.S.A. Main imports: food, manufactures, machinery, petroleum. Main suppliers: U.S.A., N.Z.

Churches:

Congregational	16,500
Roman Catholic	6,000
Methodist	2,000
Mormon	3,000
Seventh Day Adventist	600

COOK ISLANDS

Area: 233 sq.km. Fifteen inhabited and some 100 smaller uninhabited islands in two clusters, Northern Cook Islands and Southern Cook Islands. **Capital:** Avarua on Rarotonga Island. **Population:** 19,000, with 20,000 living in N.Z. **Government:** independent democracy, with free association with N.Z. **Economy:** Main industries: agriculture (coconuts, citrus, vegetables), citrus juice. Main exports: citrus juice, copra, bananas, tomatoes. Main markets: N.Z., Australia. Main imports: meat, dairy products, manufactures. Main suppliers: N.Z., Japan, Hong Kong, U.K., Australia.

Churches:

Cook Is. Christian Church	14,250
Seventh Day Adventist	2,500
Roman Catholic	2,250

NAURU

Area: 21.1 sq.km. One island. **Population:** 7,700. **Government:** republic with President and elected parliament of 18. **Economy:** Main industries: phosphate mining, handicrafts. Main exports: phosphates. Main markets: Australia, N.Z., Japan. Main imports: timber, building materials, foodstuffs, motor vehicles, drapery, footwear, pharmaceuticals. Main suppliers: Australia, U.K., N.Z., Hong Kong.

Churches:

Congregational	2,331
Independent (Pentecostal)	N.A.
Roman Catholic	1,268

TUVALU

Area: 25.7 sq.km. Nine atolls and islands. Mamumea, Funafuti, Vaitupu, Niutao, Nukufetau, Nanumanga, Nui, Nukulaelae. **Capital:** Funafuti. **Population:** 7,357 plus 1,500 in Nauru and Kiribati. **Government:** Independent democracy. **Economy:** Main industries: copra, fishing. Main export: copra. Main market: U.K. Main imports: foodstuffs, manufactures, petroleum. Main suppliers: Australia.

Churches:

Protestant	7,136
Seventh Day Adventist	150
Roman Catholic	Some
Jehovah's Witnesses	Some

Other religions:

Bahai	Some

KIRIBATI

Area: 684 sq.km. Thirty inhabited and some 300 uninhabited islands. Gilbert Group (16 main islands), Phoenix group (eight), Line Islands, Ocean Island. **Capital:** Tarawa on Tarawa Island in Gilbert Group. **Population:** 56,452 (Includes 3,500 Polynesians and Micronesians). **Government:** independent — elected President and House of Assembly. **Economy:** Main industries: phosphate mining, agriculture (copra, taro, fruit, vegetables), fisheries, livestock, handicrafts. Main exports: phosphate, copra. Main markets: Australia, N.Z., U.K. Main imports: foodstuffs, machinery and transport equipment, manufactures, mineral fuels. Main suppliers: Australia, U.K.

Churches:

Roman Catholic	28,321
Kiribati Protestant	24,726
Seventh Day Adventist	893
Pentecostal	517
Mormon	100

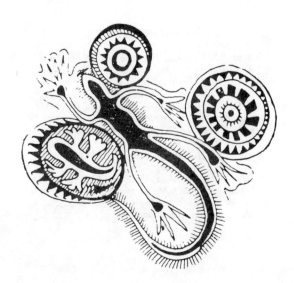

Culture My Culture

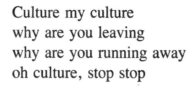

Culture my culture
why are you leaving
why are you running away
oh culture, stop stop

I need you culture
I want you
to be with me
to remain with me

for *sukwe*
and for *lagia*
for *mateana*
and for feasting

Culture
please my culture
come back
come back to me

Destroy the western
stop him growing
burn him down
for he's killing you

Oh culture
oh my culture
come back
I need you
and I'll die with you

Albert Leomala

From *Mana*. Used by permission.
Note: In North Pentecost dialect, *sukwe* is a pig killing ceremony, *lagia* is a
marriage ceremony, and *mateana* is a funeral ceremony.

PART THREE:

SING OUT STRONG

Editor's Note: There are two methods of communicating effectively throughout the Pacific: speeches (sing out strong) and gathering around the fire (story yarning). The statements, poetry and song in this section present a variety of issues that have been raised by Pacific people.

The women's statements are taken from the 1975 Women's Conference, "Women Speak Out." The conference was sponsored by the Pacific Conference of Churches, the YWCA and the University of the South Pacific.

Bishop Gregory Singkai and Dr. Alexius Sarei spoke to a conference at Bougainville, Papua New Guinea, in 1976 as the struggle for national unity was still going on. They stood in opposition to the national government, which was at that time headed by Michael Somare.

The poem by Senator Moses Uludong raises the question of imperialism for Americans in the United States in very personal terms. The statements of John and Julian Anjain and Senator Uludong, given before a State Department commission investigating the continuing effects of U.S. atomic testing at the Bikini Atoll, open for us the human tragedy of the nuclear age in the Pacific.

Father Walter Lini, prime minister of Vanuatu, addresses the United Nations upon the admission of Vanuatu as the organization's 155th member state. The song which ends this section is the new national anthem of Vanuatu. It is printed in Bislama, which is the neo-Melanesian pidgin of Vanuatu. You will be able to understand most of its meaning by hearing "ni Vanuatu" phonetically sung out strong.

37

1

2

1. (L to R): Fr. Cherubim Dambui, the Rev. Fred Timakata,
deputy prime minister of Vanuatu, and Utula Samana.
Dambui and Samana are heads of provincial governments
in Papua New Guinea.

2. Old names — and ways — yield as independence heralds new
beginnings for Pacific nations.

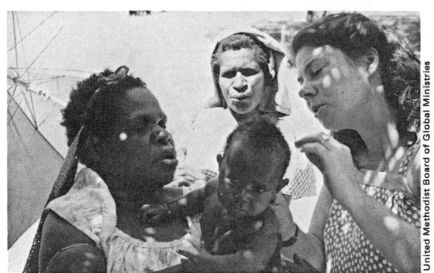

United Methodist Board of Global Ministries
by John C. Goodwin

3

B. David Williams, Jr.

4

B. David Williams, Jr.

5

3. *Nutrition education is stressed by this midwife as she works with Pacific mothers and children.*

4. *Polynesian schoolgirls demonstrate the Pacific Islanders' love of music and dance.*

5. *Micronesians of Saipan, Commonwealth of the Northern Marianas, in a community meeting react to a Japanese plan to dump radioactive wastes in the northwest Pacific.*

WOMEN SPEAK OUT

Tupou Fanua from Tonga.

Religion is to me a personal thing, a faith that shapes a woman's life. To me, religion is God living in your heart, and he living in your heart will rule from there. And I sincerely believe that we will never go wrong if we have that administration from within us.

In Tonga, religion has played quite a lot on women's lives. It has given us freedom. You see, I think from all the Pacific Islands we all had religions in some kind of way. We were groping around in a dark room, touching a chair, feeling and thinking that was something suitable for a God. With us it was like that. When Christianity was brought in and our King was converted, our people welcomed it. There was a great change; there was freedom in the land. And not only from the higher ranks but from all ranks.

What I think about now is that we might get too narrow-minded about religion; that our minds may be taken up too much with religion in the old gospel — I mean religion in the Old Testament — and not with the New Testament. And what is the leading spirit of all is love. If we women could learn to love each other, to love your husband, and your children, to love people as you do yourself, as the Bible says, which is the compass for Christian religion—that, I think, will solve all problems.

Akaiti Ama from Cook Islands.

I speak as a Cook Islander and as a member of the Cook Islands Christian Church of the Ngatangiia Parish. I am also a promoter and organizer of the World Day of Prayer services in the Cook Islands and president of the Rarotonga CICC Women's Council.

The four main denominations in the Cook Islands are the Cook Islands Christian Church, Roman Catholic, Seventh Day Adventist and the Church of the Latter Day Saints (Mormons).

Religion plays a very important part in the life of most Cook Islanders, men and women. In the CICC, men have an advantage over women, and I hear that this is the

same in the Roman Catholic Church and the Seventh Day Adventist Church.

In the CICC, all the ministers of the twenty-two parishes are men. Not one is a woman. In each parish there are between twelve (at the most) and six (at the least) deacons. Only two women in the CICC parishes are deaconesses in their own right. One is from Mauke Island and the other is from Ngatangiia, Rarotonga.

Further, women do not preach from the pulpit—only men do that. I often wonder why this is so, especially since women clean and sweep the pulpit. If only men are allowed to preach from the pulpit, then why can't they sweep and clean it?

In the Cook Islands, women have to wear hats or cover their hair whenever they have to enter a church. Women do all the preparations for any feast at a religious function and wait on the guests. After the feast the women have to clean up. The men decide the feast but the women do all the work. Women have accepted this and the men took advantage of them. I think it's about time we do something about it.

There are many other ways in which women do all or most of the work in the church. Yet to hold a position in the church, for example, to be a deacon, one must: a) be a man, b) be an elderly person, and c) preferably be a chief traditionally or a son of a chief.

Another interesting thing about deacons and ministers is that if their wives die, they cannot remain as ministers or deacons because they have no wife to do all the woman's duties. Unless he marries again, he will lose his position. In our church at Ngatangiia, the deacons' wives clean all the utensils used for Holy Communion.

This goes back to our traditional culture which, with Western culture, has a great influence on religion in the Cook Islands. For example, only the wife of a minister or deacon can sweep the pulpit, which is a throwover from when the wives of the early missionaries did this. The influence from traditional culture comes in from only sons having access to titles, not daughters, for example.

Most men like to stick to these traditions, but it is simply a way of preventing women from becoming ministers or deacons. Thus, women can be ordinary members of the church, but not its organizers or leaders. I think it's about time we do something about it. We will speak out!

Gregoria Baty from Guam.

Guam is predominantly a Catholic island and this religion tends to shape women in the image of the Virgin Mary, a pure and humble mother and wife. Although

parents tell their daughters this on Guam, illegitimacy is quite high. One out of nine children is born out of wedlock. This problem had been taken care of by the extended family during the old days. Now the nuclear families have left a lot of children neglected and unloved. They grow up criminals, delinquents, or if they get married, they grow up as bad parents.

Certain effective family planning methods are proscribed by the Catholic Church. Well, men and women go to church on Sunday, but on Monday the woman has the choice of getting her free birth control pill at the Department of Health or getting an abortion at the Public Hospital if she needs to, and usually she is free to make this choice. Unfortunately, abortion is not covered by her insurance because the legislature, mainly made up of men, were pressured by the Catholic bishop to write a contract by the insurance company not to include abortion among a woman's medical benefits. That's a fact.

Ida Teariki-Bordes from Tahiti.

I want to ask a question to all the women from the other Islands. A very important question in Tahiti is religion. Nearly everybody is religious, either Catholic or Protestant or Mormon. The more important religion is Protestantism, and the Catholics coming after, Adventists next and then the Mormons. I want to know if the pastors and priests in your Islands have taken a position socially on economics and politics. In Tahiti we have a very special problem, which is the bomb, and we should like to know if in your countries your pastors and your priests take a position on all these subjects.

The time I want to tell you about is when John, my brother, was the deputy in the French National Assembly, and he was against the bomb. As he is a very religious man (he's Protestant), he thought he would get help from the pastors and even from the Catholic bishop, so he went to see them. And that was just to help the Tahitians . . . . So he went to see the bishop first and the bishop said: "I can't speak against France because I'm French and I don't want to speak anything against my own government." So my brother phoned us and said, "Please, can't you do something?" (because I live about 40 miles from the main town of Papeete). "Please, would you try to see the priests in your place, because your husband is a Catholic, and ask the priest if he could help us."

So I went to the priest and after a small talk I began to direct the conversation to nuclear tests and the priest was so afraid to talk about it that he just ran out, forgetting his hat in the house! He was so afraid to say a word about

that. So I told my husband what it was and he said that this was a French priest and maybe the bishop had told him not to talk about the bomb. So now there was nothing to do, so I decided to turn to my Protestant pastors.

I was not happy about the result because, first, they are Tahitians. And so I couldn't understand when the Protestant pastors would not talk about the bomb. I said, "We are women and we are thinking about our children, and you should think about our children too." But the Protestant pastor explained to me that they were afraid to talk about it because just a little while before one of the French Protestant pastors had talked about and against the bomb and he was sent right away back to France. So they were afraid to talk.

That's the question I want to ask you. Why are priests afraid to talk about all these things against the bomb? They represent God and God wants the good of the people, and they should want the good of the people too. And I want to know if this is the same in your countries, if the priests take the same position and don't want to be involved.

This year it's a bit better because the bishop wrote an article in which he says, very vaguely, I must say, a little against the atom bomb. And the Protestants are talking a little bit more. But I must explain that I didn't know about the South Pacific Bishops' meetings [the World Bishops' Conference, Vatican, 1975] in which the bishops decided against all these things. So the bishop in Tahiti had to write something about this and say something, but it was very, very mild.

I didn't realize about the conference because in Tahiti we have *no* contact with the outside world. They cut it off. Everything is turned to outside, to Europe.

But this doesn't mean that I'm no more Protestant. I'm still a very good Protestant and my husband is still a very good Catholic because the religion is God's; the pastors and priests are human beings.

Grace Mera from New Hebrides.

I'd like to answer the question that our sister from Tahiti has posed. She would like to know from us—from other countries—what our ministers' or our churches' stand is in relation to the bomb and nuclear testing in Tahiti.

I am very grateful that this Conference has made it possible for people from New Caledonia, New Hebrides and Tahiti to meet, as we share a common area—we are French Territories. We come under French colonialism, and this particular system makes it very, very difficult for our three peoples to meet, to communicate. As our Tahitian sister has stated, information to come out is very difficult and the relevant information to come in to us is also very difficult. This is the first time that I am able to hear anything from a Tahitian.

In the New Hebrides, as far as Christian religion is concerned, we have something like a dozen different denominations of one kind of Christianity or another. I have been brought up in the Anglican tradition, my father being an Anglican minister. I went through Anglican church schools and have been involved in church activities.

The point is this: in the New Hebrides we have not had the education; we were denied education. People were educated by the different churches, but what they were taught were only Christian teachings and maybe how to read and write. So any knowledge of anything outside the religious traditions they don't know very much about. For example, a worldview or a world outlook, anything on economics, and things like this, many people do not understand because they have not had the chance to be educated.

Coming back to our ministers, in the Anglican Church in the New Hebrides we have between sixty and eighty priests, and out of these only two have had high school education. They did not have high school education because the government made it impossible for them to have this. They had schooling because their families made it possible for them. Therefore, many of our ministers, because of lack of education, do not understand much about politics, economics or, as you said, the bomb. However, a few priests who understand the world problems and the world situation as it is today are involved in political developments like some of you might have heard about in the New Hebrides. There are a number of political parties now, one of them being the National Party, which is headed by and has a core from the church from the different denominations. Much of the leadership are ministers.

Our stand is with you. We are against the bomb. We are against militarism in the Pacific.

However, our voice is not yet a united voice because the few who understand are so few, and our people who are the masses are so much for us to cope with that the information has not been channeled back into the grassroots effectively yet. But the few who have had the chance to be educated or to see this light realize that that is the challenge. And we hope more will come to understand that we must stand together. Things like militarism and other aspects that arise from it I think we have to

handle carefully and maybe base our ideas on real Christianity—not the Christianity that has been created after Christ dies, but Christ's *true* teaching, has to be involved.

Dewe Gorodey from New Caledonia.

I'm from New Caledonia, which is a French territory like Tahiti. We have a situation similar to the New Hebrides but very different from some of yours, because we are under a colonial system.

In New Caledonia the priests and the ministers are going along with the colonial system. They are supporting it. My Tahitian sister was saying that the bishop refused to take a stand against the nuclear tests. I was not surprised because it is exactly the same in New Caledonia. When you know that the people who have come to speak of God perpetrate the colonial system, you ask yourself if they really represent God.

Salvadora Katosang from Micronesia.

I would like to say that the Tahitian people are not alone in their struggles to stop the nuclear testing in Tahiti.

These are the statistics right now: between 1946 and 1958, the United States detonated 93 bombs of all sorts, including the hydrogen bombs, on the island of Kwajalein. Thus far, the people are the only ones who have been struggling to free the Pacific, especially Micronesia, from these tests.

They have not involved the priests and the ministers of the various denominations, simply because priests and ministers are considered nonpolitical people, although they probably could help along those lines in the name of helping people as people of God. For that reason we have not involved the priests or the ministers. But rather, we have tried to work among the native people only.

Ti Harawira from New Zealand.

I'd like to comment on the question of religion. I'd like to say again that religion for my people has not only affected them but has totally screwed them up, and today our young people not only reject religion but also reject the education system as a whole.

I belong to the Ngapuri tribe which is from the north of Auckland, up. Ours strayed from the main tribe. The missionaries came to our tribe and they taught us how to do away with any carvings at all, because my people were made to believe that they were carved in the image of some of the evil people, of evil spirits and the devil. So they did away with this beautiful culture.

This is how religion had affected my people and is still affecting them today. The churches own more land in the Ngapuri area than my people. We were made to believe

that if you prayed long enough and you look up to God while the white man takes your land, you will get to heaven. This is what happened and is still happening today.

Dewe Gorodey from New Caledonia.

As for the missionaries, none of them could possibly conceive of the fact that Jesus Christ could be colored and a woman. . . . They are pleased to present us with a pure white and civilized God. Just before 1853, it was an archbishop called Douarre who intervened with Napoleon III to have the French government take possession of New Caledonia, for above all, it must not be left to the English and to their pastors of the Mission Society of London. After that, these missionaries dare come to us insinuating that it is a sin to get involved in politics, that to demand one's land is to cry vengeance, hate and violence, that one must love one's enemy as oneself. I answer them that from the moment they do not take issue with the colonial system, they justify it. And to justify a governmental system is to get involved in politics.

Violence! As it is, they who did not hesitate to massacre the Kanaks with guns in order to implant their Christianity in my country, while he of whom they claim to speak, Christ, let himself be crucified peacefully—it is they, along with the administrators, the military and the settlers, who have imposed violence on my people, stealing their land and annihilating their culture.

Konai Helu Thaman from Tonga.

When we are talking about religion, we are, without knowing it, talking about the introduced religion that has pervaded all the Islands. Very few of us have mentioned the traditional religion. So it goes to show that we have been thoroughly socialized in the Western religion and we therefore have come to accept some of the Western values. We can no longer differentiate this from our traditional religion. We have incorporated some of these Western religious values and even have called this our own.

The second thing that has come out is the great influence of religion in shaping lives, our women's roles, so that in effect religion, the Christian religion especially, has reinforced the social patterns, has reinforced the traditional patterns, that we have been used to. And I think that it has become evident that some of these norms, some of these rules that have been introduced by this Western religion have been constructive—we can certainly do with a bit of love, we can certainly do with a bit of unity that Christianity preaches. But some of these norms as they have been pointed out, have tended to restrict us women from developing our full potential.

"WE ARE A GROUP OF FOOLS"

Alexius Sarei

We are a group of fools trying to attempt the impossible. Trying to make people realize what they are—human; what they are about—living in complete self-respect; where they are going—growing and developing with dignity. We believe (and we are mostly ex-priests, seminarians and priests) that humanity comes first. Unless we keep this at the center of our thinking, we are useless with and for our people.

People see us as radical and call us power hungry. Ridiculous! Leaders must stand up for their people and their rights. I must confess that the first people to scream at us and dump us were church people, the same ones who taught us to value human dignity and stand up for the rights of people—those who as missionaries preach justice and show Christ. As a former priest I must say that a majority of priests today, but not all, are pharisees.

They have had their day. Now it is time for them to shut up or get out.

That was the religious aspect. Now for the political. In the last four years here as district commissioner, and head of the now suspended provincial government, I have learned that service to the people cannot be divided, because people cannot be divided. They are whole human beings. The religious and political leaders have the same vocation: to serve the people.

We are only ten people in our leadership team. And eight are former priests, or in seminary training, or priests. But we have the people who are taking over their own governing. Village government, which is basically our cultural Big Man system, has been renewed. It has developed and has succeeded in giving decision making back to the village. We have undone what the church and

the government did to us in the past hundred years. Our people are no longer afraid or dependent. Our Big Men are again proud of our cultural heritage.

But it is a hard job to say again, "Okay, Big Men, you go ahead and make the decisions with your people. You do not have to only listen and say 'yes' to the Klap" (this refers to expatriate government officials). Giving back responsibility to people who have been made dependent is not easy. There is a loss of resilience and people are less willing to question what is put before them. Leadership by birth (i.e., recognized natural leaders) rather than leadership by election must be reestablished. Our natural leaders have been replaced by ineffectual councilors. Village governments are now replacing local councils as these councils die a natural death.

Our culture is still rich. We have our feet on the ground while Western culture has gone to the moon! Unless human beings have their feet on the ground, they are nothing. Our people are coming around to see that they are something. They can contribute to and control their destiny. People need freedom and we are giving them freedom to create their own structures. We leaders have purposely given our people no directions. They must learn to use their own power. Why standardize all the time? This is another area of overdependence. What is needed now is a loosening-up process to help people to think and talk together and decide on their own pattern of living; to be involved in decision making and not just hammering nails.

In the late fifties there was a craze for projects. People were not involved. They were not people's projects, but the priests' projects. The people were made dependent on the priests. The priests decided the projects while the people did the work. The projects all failed when the priests left because people had no experience with decision making. It was the same with the public service: you saw the local officers hanging on the district commissioner and not given real responsibility. Where people are not given responsibility you cannot blame them when they cannot carry on the work. So we are encouraging village assemblies. These are built in our own local fashion, and they are a symbol of local power, of our local ways. The same with village art and culture. Life depends on culture and tradition.

But do not think that our movement is only a return to the past. On the modern level we have started the Bougainville Development Corporation. I admit that in the past two years we have crossed the border from what we want to do, to what we do not want to be: we are becoming a capitalistic concern. We wanted to acquire the assets of our people before someone else got them. In BougAir, in shipping, in canteens, in catering, in timber, in food production, in plantations, we control our assets and intend to spread them among our people. In becoming a capitalistic company with 555,000 shares we hope to contain within our island the money generated for the needs and development of our people.

People accuse us of being greedy and selfish. This is not a movement to get control of the mine; it started long before the mine. Its aim is to recapture for the people their right to take part in their own decision making. For those of you who don't have a mine, I hope you never have one. We are fighting world opinion because money is not the aim of life. Human relationship is what we are trying to achieve for our people.

Human relationships are more powerful than the atomic bomb. A united nation is meaningless unless people on the village and clan level have human dignity. What is the use of trying to unite, if first of all we do not accept one another as human beings? We cannot be part of Papua New Guinea while the tribes there keep on fighting. There must be acceptance as human beings. This is the fault of the government and the missions. They have had great power for good, but did not use it.

The Christian churches have not tried to influence the government to work for real justice among the people. I am convinced that bishops and priests have real moral power. God has said that he is with them. What are they afraid of? The churches are afraid to stand up. Their excuse is that they must not get involved in politics. The bishops of our church met recently in Rabaul and their only statement was about drink. What baby talk! Why can't bishops, priests, politicians make statements about justice and human dignity? Somare and his leaders are Christians. Why can't they use their power for justice and human dignity?

In the Catholic Church's self-study people were asked what is wrong. There is nothing wrong with the people. It's the leaders. They won't use their power for good, for the good of the people. As an ex-priest I must say I am sorry; but I left the priesthood because I could not exercise my moral power as I can now.

We see our approach here as a model not only for us, but for our nation, and for the Pacific as a whole. Before we come forth and hold hands with others here and throughout the Pacific, we need to succeed at establishing ourselves here. Then in the natural process of things we can join with others in growth and human development. It will have to spread. The soul of unity must come, but we need to establish our own strength first.

"HERE IS MY STAND"

Gregory Singkai

Since I was so recently appointed in 1974, I have already got into trouble. First I toured the diocese and listened to the people. So many people kept asking me, "Bishop, are you on our side, or on Somare's side?" I kept referring this to Father Momis, our resident politician, and tried to stay neutral.

As Papua New Guinea's Independence Day came near in 1975, our people said, "Let's celebrate *our* Independence early to show the world that we are not with the Somare government." On that day I joined my people and spoke on the occasion. I said, "When you build a nation you must build it with God." Immediately the press rushed at me to find my position. I was full up with Bougainville politics so I let it all out. I announced where I stood. The press said, "Bishop Gregory announces the Catholic Church's support of the *illegal* Bougainville secessionist movement." People were on me like blowflies. The bishops who were scared by Somare came at me. Somare said that I could be considered guilty of treason for my stand. My reply to the press was that this *illegal* movement had to be proved so. I do not believe that it is.

Let me tell you my reasons for taking my stand. The individual person is very important. The importance of the human person is a basic Christian idea. The government must respect that. Also, a person's right to independence is sacred. For a person is free. The Bougainville movement differs with the government here because the government has failed to put this properly in the Constitution. The PNG government has not taken seriously human dignity and respect for the individual's rights, desires and concerns.

I do not oppose the Papua New Guinea government altogether, but only in respect to its denial of the person's right to independence. The PNG government has failed in its withdrawal of the chapter on provincial government from the Constitution. No chance has been given to us to develop ourselves. I do not like the top to give directions all the time.

I looked at international law, since Australia and the United Nations were against us. I saw that under the trust territory regulations, those who are responsible for us should bring us to the stage where the wishes of the people must be followed. As far as I am concerned, we didn't break any law. When we wanted to make our decision, those holding our trust relationship would not listen to us. It cannot be proved from any existing law that my stand was illegal. You can look at the United Nations charter, and you will find nothing there to prove that the Bougainville movement is illegal. And the Constitution of Papua New Guinea was not yet officially promulgated.

Finally, I took my stand because my people wanted this, and the other churches also agreed. The leaders of my people and I hold the same beliefs and principles. Our people must be led by leaders who will lead and stand up for their principles. We will fail if we do not lead our people.

I have supported and worked with the leaders of *our* government here. I believe the Somare government has imposed itself on Bougainville by going against its own Eight Point Plan and disregarding the human dignity of all our people. As for the missionaries, I would not call them hypocrites. I know that they are people of different cultures and with ways different from ours. They are in a culture which is so different from their own. They must be led and helped by our own people. Also, we have to understand that they are in a difficult position. The Somare government could easily expel them if they stood up.

Here is my stand.

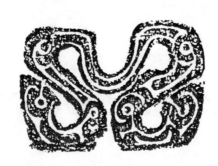

Milking The Natives

I never invited you
but you came to my island
and I welcomed you

You told me
I was a savage
and I believed you

You told me I was doomed to hell
and I was scared
you gave me your bible
and I prayed

You told me to till my island
I planted coconuts for your profits
you told me to dig holes and bunkers and
I defended you with my life and land
but you bombed my house and my land
and I ran into the woods

You told me
you freed me from your war
and I should be grateful
to you as my liberator

You established your government
on my island
without my permission

You sent me to your school
and I learned your way
and I worked for you as an office boy
you gave me your dollars
and I bought your things

Now you tell me
I cannot live without
your money
your way
your things
and I believe you

But I can only get them
if I give you my island and freedom
Never!!!

Moses Ymal Uludong

From *Mana*. Used by permission.

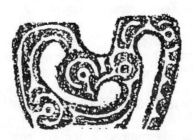

Nuclear Testing by the United States: Its Bitter Aftermath

John Anjain

I come from Rongelap Atoll in the Marshall Islands. Rongelap is one of the three atolls that was severely affected by radiation from the atomic and hydrogen bomb tests which were done by the United States in the last part of the 1940s and the early part of the 1950s. More than sixty atomic bombs were tested at Bikini and Eniwetok.

On March 1, 1954, the United States exploded the first and largest of the hydrogen bombs that were to be tested on the island of Bikini, which is about 125 miles west of Rongelap. This test, which was called Bravo, caused great damage to the islands of Rongelap and Utirik. On that day, we saw a flash of lightning in the west like a second sun rising. We heard a loud explosion and within minutes the ground began to shake. A few hours later the radioactive fallout began to drop on the people, into the drinking water and on the food. The children played in the colorful, ash-like powder. They did not know what it was and many erupted on their arms and faces. We were not evacuated from the island for more than two days, although twenty-eight Americans on another island nearby were removed within twenty-four hours. Our people began to be very sick. They vomited, burns showed on their skin and people's hair began to fall out.

Since then, the people of Rongelap in particular have experienced the most severe radiation problems. In 1957, the American Atomic Energy Commission doctors told us that our home island was completely safe for us to return. Even though they said that there was no radiation on the island, I'm sorry to say now that ever since that time we've returned to home, many of us have experienced diseases that we did not experience before. Over the past few years, an alarming number of exposed people, as well as the nonexposed who returned in 1957, have had thyroid cancer and radiation-related diseases. Nineteen out of the twenty-two children who were born on Rongelap during the fallout have had thyroid surgery. Nine of the nonexposed have also had thyroid operations. We are told that many more will be operated on in the years ahead.

This leads us only to believe that surely our islands are not quite as safe as the Department of Energy said they are. My son Lekoj was only one year old when he was exposed to the fallout in 1954. He grew up so strong and healthy that I thought nothing would ever happen to him, but in late 1972 he began to be very sick and the doctor said he had a very dangerous disease called leukemia. He died just a few weeks later in November 1972.

Most of you have heard that the people of Bikini have been removed again from their home island because it is not safe for them to live there. In 1969, however, the AEC told the Bikinians that their atoll was safe and that there was virtually no radiation left on Bikini. It is really sad to say that these people are now contaminated and will probably never go back to their home island again. In November 1978 the Department of Energy did a radiation survey over the northern part of the Marshall Islands. According to this survey, we are told that the level of radiation on Rongelap, especially in the northern part of the atoll, is higher than the level of radiation on Eniwetok and on Bikini, which is said to be off-limits for twenty years to the people there.

We are told by the DOE doctors not to eat the food on the land or the fish in the ocean near these islands. Coconut crab, which is considered one of our best delicacies, is no longer edible because of the great amount of radiation in it. It is very sad and discouraging not to be able to eat our own food nor to live on many of our islands. But more alarming is the fact that we have been eating the food and living on these islands since the AEC told us it was safe in 1957. We wonder what new problems we will suffer from these exposures. If this DOE survey is accurate, we the people of Rongelap would like to know why the country of the United States is not doing anything for the people of Rongelap. Is it possible that the DOE has not fully informed the Congress about their findings? It seems that the DOE is not interpreting adequately the meaning of their findings concerning the people of Rongelap.

For these reasons and many others, I have come a long way here to testify in this hearing. I wish to present a few proposals to this hearing and ask your recommendation on them. First, we the people of Rongelap need independent doctors and scientists who can look into the radiation problems that have affected our islands. We believe that these people will not only find out true meaning or true information, but that the Congress of the United States will consider their findings. Second, we request

the U.S. Congress to immediately provide compensation for the Rongelap and Utirik people who have had thyroid surgery but were not on the island during the fallout. And third, we request the U.S. Congress to provide immediate compensation for islands that are now considered to be contaminated.

And for myself, I would like to say that the government of the United States is making a big mistake in returning the people of Eniwetok to Eniwetok. I think that the island is very much contaminated and that people should not go there. Thank you.

Mendelsohn: Thank you very much for the statement and thank you very much also for traveling this great distance to join us today. I'm sure everyone here appreciates it. There is a chance for some questions and comments, and there is with us today Glenn Alcalay, a Ph.D. candidate at Rutgers, who is working on radiation effects on the Marshall Islands, who can help in answering questions. Are there some questions? Yes, Hilda Mason.

Mason: You made reference to compensation for the contamination. How would you compensate for the contamination of the islands?

Julian Anjain: Yes, the northern part of Rongelap is considered to be very much contaminated and the DOE doctors tell us not to go there because it's very hot, and the food there, we're not to eat it. And we feel that we should have compensation for the loss of our land.

Mendelsohn: That means that compensation has not been given yet?

Julian Anjain: Yes.

Mendelsohn: Yes, Dr. Lifton.

Lifton: I would like to ask any of the three witnesses more about what has happened to the Islanders as a community, as a people, as a consequence of the fallout problem and the nuclear radiation.

Julian Anjain: Glenn Alcalay, who is an ex-Peace Corps, spent so many years in the Marshall Islands, he probably could answer you.

Alcalay: I was a Peace Corps volunteer on Utirick, one of the irradiated atolls, from 1975 through 1977, and right now I'm doing research on the anthropological and sociological dislocation problems resulting from the radiation in the Marshall Islands. I think the best answer to Dr. Lifton's question is the statement by one of the Brookhaven doctors that was in charge of the medical and radiological examinations in the Marshalls and who has recently said he feels the sociologic and anthropologic dislocations may be more serious than the actual radiation pathologies in terms of the people having been moved from island to island, in terms of their having lost their ancestral homelands. And he cited current statistics in the Marshalls that show that the Marshalls have one of the highest suicide rates in the world, and they have a very high rate of alcoholism, juvenile delinquency, family disruptions, etc. — all of the usual things connected with a broken culture. And my first hand experience with interviews on Utirick had to do with the people attributing many of their problems to the radiation. Most of their physiological problems now are believed to be directly related to the radiation effects, and things like common colds, head colds, muscle aches now are believed by these people to be related to the radiation. So the manifestations are quite deep and long term.

Mendelsohn: Thank you. Yes, Dr. Morgan.

Morgan: How many cases of thyroid nodules and thyroid carcinoma have been detected among these Marshallese so far?

Alcalay: On Rongelap, where the scientists believe they received 175 rads, out of 22 children who were under the age of 12 at the time of irradiation, 19 of these have thyroid neoplasa. On Utirick they have a total of 20 people out of the original population. These figures actually don't reflect the true nature of the effects in the sense that a lot of people have died and it's not clear whether their deaths were related to the radiation. The Marshallese custom does not allow for autopsy, so a lot of these deaths, many in fact, have been due to the radiation; but these are the ones that are counted by the Brookhaven National Laboratory doctors and scientists, and they have tended over the years to be very conservative. They have continued to underplay and minimize the effects of the radiation in the Marshalls. So, in answer to your question, these are the known cases of thyroid.

Mendelsohn: Thank you. Are there other questions or comments?

Lifton: One more brief comment about what Dr. Alcalay just said. Where people have fears after radiation exposure that any ordinary occurrence, a common cold, what have you, may be caused by radiation, there's always a temptation on the part of restitution- or potentially restitution-paying agencies to say, Aha, it's a false idea, it's not due to radiation. But the point is the whole picture, the whole syndrome, the whole constellation of fear is due precisely to the radiation exposure; one has to understand that.

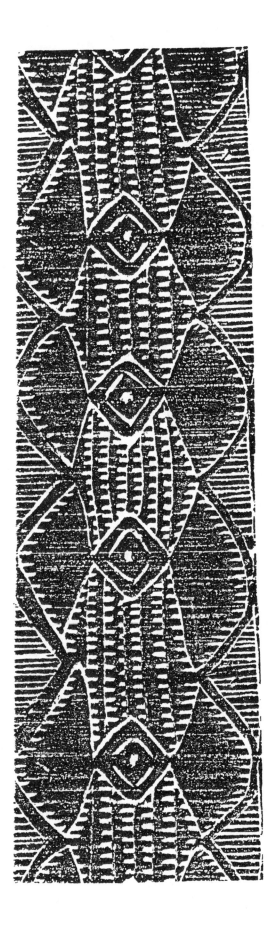

A Nuclear-Free Pacific

Moses Ymal Uludong

Among the countries located in the Pacific, there is one subject most important to us all—that of a Nuclear-Free Pacific. Representatives of our organization have attended and participated in conferences in the last several years throughout the region on this issue: the Suva Conference of 1975, the 1978 Ponape Conference, the meeting held in Hawaii in 1980 and the annual antinuclear bomb conferences in Japan. It is timely and appropriate that labor unions in the Pacific, the most potent and true representatives of the poor and ordinary citizens of our countries, get involved in the movement as a force in itself.

In these regional meetings, we met and talked with people and groups fighting for the same cause in their countries. The information we learned, the contacts we made and the solidarity we established strengthen our resolve and encourage us to continue the struggle in our country.

The sufferings of our brothers and sisters in the Marshalls from the American testing, the contamination of the Polynesian Islands by the French tests, the U.S. intention to store nuclear waste on a Pacific island and the Japanese plan to dump nuclear wastes in the Pacific Ocean all contribute to and provide more reasons for the inclusion of a nuclear-free provision in our Constitution when it was written in 1979. Article XIII, Section 6, states:

> Harmful substances such as nuclear, chemical, gas or biological weapons intended for use in warfare, nuclear power plants and waste materials therefrom, shall not be used, tested, stored or disposed of within the territorial jurisdiction of Palau without the express approval of not less than three-fourths of the votes cast in a referendum submitted on this specific question.

The territorial jurisdiction of Palau extends from the outer reefs 200 miles out and around the 241 islands, bordering with territorial waters of Papua New Guinea and Indonesia to the south, Philippines to the west and Federated States of Micronesia to the north and east. This restriction in our constitution took effect on January 1, 1981. The U.S. government for two years, in 1979 and 1980, tried to nullify our constitution due to this provision; however, our people stood firm. In three separate referenda, the people of Palau ratified the constitution by an over 75 percent majority, probably the only constitution in the world that went three votings.

The U.S. government is now employing different tactics to evade our nuclear-free constitution. The United States is negotiating with our government for a treaty called Free Association Compact, which if implemented would suspend that provision in exchange for fifteen-year financial aid. It is possible that this document can be put up for a plebiscite this year and that our people will be blackmailed into supporting it or face the loss of U.S. financial aid. Our people, I am sure, with your support, will weather this storm as we have done in the last two years. I believe our constitution is the first in the world that addresses this issue of banning all nuclear materials, including weapons and wastes, and should serve as an example to all progressive peoples, groups and countries who desire genuine peace and harmony in the world.

There is an ominous dark cloud hanging overhead, that is, the Japanese government project to dump nuclear wastes in the Pacific. It has been suspended this year but is said to be planned for next year. Peoples, leaders, organizations and governments throughout the Pacific have expressed vehement opposition to this plan. Our National Congress last year and this year adopted a resolution opposing the plan. One of the leaders of our organization, who is also a member of our Congress, was in Japan last week accompanying the governor of Northern Marianas in presenting a formal and legal petition to the Japanese parliament against the plan. If Japan proceeds with the project next year then we have no choice but to consider some concrete action.

I propose that we discuss these alternatives:
1. Get our governments to ban importation of Japanese goods.
2. Prohibit Japanese boats from fishing in our waters.
3. Boycott Japanese products.
4. Refuse to handle cargoes to and from Japan.
5. Not allow Japanese tourists into our countries.

I know the above proposals will have direct and adverse effects in our countries, but when the very future of the region is at stake, we must take strong and decisive actions if we are to survive. Our region has been abused enough.

VANUATU ENTERS THE UNITED NATIONS

Walter Hadye Lini

My delegation is deeply honored and thankful for the many kind words expressed by various representatives at this, Vanuatu's historic occasion. It is with pride, humility and gratitude that I stand before the Assembly in the name of the people of Vanuatu, and the fact that I do so at a moment when our young republic takes its place as a State Member of the United Nations is an additional source of pride and appreciation, and I am indeed grateful for the opportunity to address the Assembly at this particular hour.

The Assembly has before it an agenda that is wholly representative of the spirit, principle and commitment of the Charter of this great Organization, which has since its birth been the hope for the emancipation of countless numbers of the human race. From such a high and honorable duty I should not wish to detain negotiations and it is my intention, therefore, to be brief in what I have to say.

Initially, I wish to confirm that my presence here is of some personal significance, for it was before this Organization's Committee of Twenty-Four that on two occasions I was granted permission to appear in order to present a case for the decolonization of my country. The chief concern and assistance of that Committee is widely regarded in Vanuatu as having made a fundamental contribution toward achieving the political freedom of our people, and that fact I gladly acknowledge now. Because of this, the United Nations has a very special place in our affections and esteem — the principal reason why we regard our membership as the most significant event since achieving nationhood.

The difficult nature of our national birth gave rise to expressions of concern by a significant number of countries represented in this Assembly, and I would take this occasion to record the debt of gratitude we owe to them. To some significant degree, the experience of Vanuatu as

the final steps down the long and difficult road to independence were taken may, I respectfully suggest, contain within it an object lesson which is totally in keeping with the essential reasons for the very existence of this council of nations, which a free Vanuatu now so proudly joins.

We are a small country located in the vastness of the world's greatest ocean, far removed from the mainstream of international attention. It was principally because of this that we fell prey to the divisive, antidemocratic and selfish attention of those who would have interrupted our progress, our political and constitutional advancement. Such negative influences may well have succeeded but for the acts of assistance constituting a collective concern of high honor which we were given by our friends in the region.

It was a classic example of a unity of purpose, of coming together in the interest of the peace and welfare of a people and a region — surely, as I remarked, the essence of the task the United Nations was formed to carry out. If at times of crisis the strong assist those who often, through no fault of their own, are unable adequately to meet the situation, then and only then will it be possible for the weak to become strong and collectively, if not individually, to stand free and able to render assistance themselves when any given circumstance demands it. . . .

Our difficult colonial past has also prompted in our national experience many concerns, and, with all humility, there may be occasions when a mutual benefit may be derived if those concerns are voiced here. It is the fact that some of our concerns are regional, based on support for what we in Vanuatu regard as a natural expectation held by those Pacific peoples still subject to colonial rule. Their right to be granted a free and unfettered political determination is a principle we shall not abdicate. We shall not forget that this principle is supported by this Assembly on every available opportunity, just as we shall advocate and strive with equal conviction to ensure that our Pacific Ocean be free from nuclear contamination through the practice of the dumping of nuclear waste or the testing of nuclear devices.

On the international scene, we shall give support with all the conviction at our command to the debate which has become known as the North-South dialogue, believing as we surely do that much depends—both in terms of justice and of international welfare—on the future relationship that will exist between the manufacturing countries and industrialized society and those who supply the basic raw materials upon which industrialized society so vitally depends. . . .

. . . the world must turn away from concepts of dominance and dependence to the reality of interdependence and to the imperatives of change that this produces. May I again suggest that the improvement in the quality of the welfare of so many who desperately need it depends on a practical recognition by industrialized society that it is in no one's long-term interest for national profit to be pursued at the expense of international poverty. The continuance of such a circumstance can only result in the inflammable structures of injustice mounting higher and higher — dread structures which do not allow half the world to earn a decent living, patterns of consumption that strain and pollute the world's resources and economic systems which benefit the few at the expense of the many.

In putting forward such concerns as and when we are able, we would hope in all sincerity that we shall be making a contribution to this Organization, to which we owe so much, while at the same time upholding and furthering the high purpose of its calling. I should like to thank the Assembly for listening so kindly and so courteously to what I have had to say.

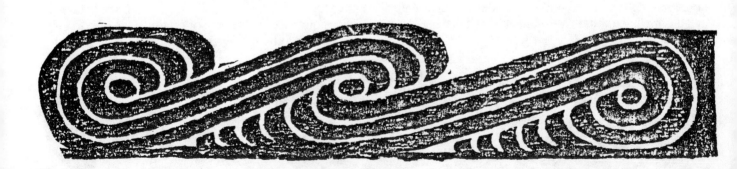

NASIONAL SINGSING BLONG VANUATU
NATIONAL ANTHEM OF VANUATU

Yumi, Yumi, Yumi i glad blong talem se
Yumi, Yumi, Yumi i man blong Vanuatu!

1. God i givim ples ia long yumi
   Yumi glat tumas long hem
   Yumi strong mo yumi tri
   long hem
   Yumi brata evriwan!

2. Plante fasin blong bifo i stap
   Plante fasin blong tedei
   Be yumi i olsem wan nomo
   Hemia fasin blong yumi!

3. Yumi save plante wok i stap
   Long ol aelan blong yumi
   God i helpem yumi evriwan
   Hemi papa blong yumi!

from the Book VANUATU
published by the University of the South Pacific
Copyright © 1980, Institute of Pacific Studies

PART FOUR:

RESPONSES FROM THE PACIFIC

Editor's Note: The following articles sample the ways in which Pacific Island leaders are dealing with the issues of the 1980s. With independence coming swiftly to the scattered island nations, much time has to be spent in seeking alliances and building unity both within the nation-states and within the region.

You have already met Bernard Narokobi, whose poem opens this book. This lawyer and dedicated Catholic lay leader from Papua New Guinea understands better than most the meaning of total human development. His work on developing the constitution for Papua New Guinea has made him a natural consultant to each nation-state to gain independence since 1974.

The Reverend Sitiveni Ratuvili is director of Social Services and Christian Citizenship of the Methodist Church of Fiji. Ratuvili has been involved in every development conference in the Pacific since 1968 and for six years was on the staff of the Development Office of the Pacific Conference of Churches.

Father Walter Lini is now the prime minister of Vanuatu. Since 1974, when he requested a leave of absence from his priestly duties in the Anglican Church, Lini has been the spokesperson for his people. From the formation of the National Pati through independence, he led the people of Vanuatu in seeking peace in the Pacific.

Yan Celené Uregei was the leader of the Legislative Assembly of New Caledonia for fourteen years. In 1977 he resigned, after a bloody demonstration, to devote full time to the independence front in New Caledonia. Uregei spends many months each year in New York seeking United Nations support for his people's cause.

This section closes with a statement from the Eglise Evangélique of New Caledonia that is a sign of fresh wind blowing in the Pacific for the 1980s.

The two poems included here are examples of the intense love of the land exhibited by Pacific Islanders and their commitment to one another. The latter comes through in Kali Vatoko's song, written during the early years of emerging National Party solidarity in Vanuatu. Vatoko is headmaster of Onesua, the secondary school run by the Presbyterian Church of Vanuatu.

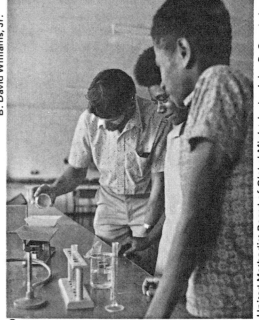

1. *Making peanut butter is demonstrated at an appropriate-technology workshop in the highlands of Papua New Guinea. Peanuts are an important source of nutrition in an area of serious malnutrition.*

2. *High school students conduct an experiment in their chemistry class.*

3. *Educating children to live in an interdependent world while preserving the best things of their own cultures is a challenge for all societies today.*

4

5

6

4. *Western influence is apparent in this department store, but note also the customer in traditional attire. K15 equals approximately U.S. $22.*

5. *Public parade in Lae, Papua New Guinea, celebrates the achievement of political independence on Sept. 15, 1975.*

6. *Yachts at anchor typify the tourist influx in the Pacific.*

PACIFIC IDENTITY AND SOLIDARITY

Bernard Narokobi

One of the greatest gifts to our people in the Pacific is that we have small, self-managing communities. From one end of this vast ocean to the other, we can safely say, even now, that we belong to relatively small communities of clans, tribes, villages, islands or units. As I travel throughout the Pacific, I never cease to marvel and rejoice at our small, self-sustained communities. Even today when we have courts, parliaments, police forces, public services and nation-states, we still have small self-governing units of people.

The Search for a Larger Solidarity

Of course, in saying that our small communities are a gift from God, I am not denying the fact that we have abused that gift, creating bitterness among ourselves or with neighboring communities. This happens when we have conflicts of one sort or another through warfare or quarrels, but it does not mean that we have lost our community belonging and solidarity.

For Christians, Christianity is the greatest Community that has been revealed, for it is first a Community of the Godhead in Trinity. Second, it is a Community of God with angels and saints who in some way are personified in the people of God on earth and in all the creatures of our creation. This is not to say that community and solidarity do not exist in non-Christian or non-Pacific communities — they do. Thus, the search for Pacific identity through a search for a definition of the "Pacific way" may result in an illusion. We may be trying to find

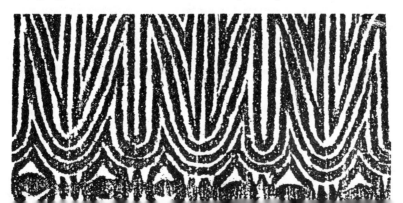

unity in practice that may or may not exist. But common historical experiences in our encounter with other races, cultures and religions may give us a common identity.

Through the Pacific Forum, our political leaders have been meeting to create a Pacific identity. Through arts festivals, our people have been meeting too, to share their cultural diversity and richness. There are other educational and economic opportunities for our people to meet as Pacific peoples to share their hopes, visions, anxieties and difficulties.

The churches, through the Pacific Conference of Churches and the Melanesian Council of Churches, have been instrumental in bringing people together.

Some Negative Forces

But not all we have learned from this coming together has been of a positive nature. Pacifique 77 was one such great opportunity for sensitive Pacific leaders to meet in Kohimarama in the Solomon Islands. There they discovered that the common experience in the Pacific is that we belong to a colonized culture or cultures. We inherit all the evils of the modern world on top of our own oppressed conditions. Our gifts and virtues are often hidden, buried under our oppression.

In our Ponape Conference, which concentrated on a Nuclear-Free Pacific and liberation struggles in the Pacific, we found that political, cultural and technological oppressions are very real in our region. From the far west we know of East Timor and the Melanesians of West Papua New Guinea struggling for their freedom. Up northwards we learn of Palauans, Guamanians (or Tumoro people), the Marianans, the Ponapeans and others searching for a place in the sun and on the ocean. We also learn of Melanesians in Vanuatu and New Caledonia struggling for self-hood and identity. In the French sphere of influence in Polynesia, we hear of struggles of self-hood and identity. The Aborigines of Australia, the Maoris of New Zealand and the native Hawaiians are all longing for self-government, for self-determination and for a place in the sun and on our vast ocean.

Even in independent countries, small natural communities are stretching and straining, twisting and turning to make adjustments between various forces and divisions. The new demands of religion, of the state, of technology, of new culture, new medicines, food, education and business enterprises are very real on our people.

A new sense of loneliness is gripping our people. Many have difficulty coping with this sense of alienation. The community we identify with continues to evaporate before our very eyes. Our villages diminish, our clans disintegrate and even our families fall apart. Further still, the church communities with which we identify for social or for genuine religious reasons begin to fall apart. Our political affiliations also fall apart when those we trust most change with political fortunes, to gain some advantage in protest against lack of material gain.

In many ways the Pacific peoples are a divided and wounded people. Physically, we are divided. Vast ocean spans, huge mountain barriers, wide river expanses and long, often rocky beaches make communication difficult. An island barely visible often seems a strange world, inhabited by gods and spirits. Today, in spite of the gifts of the written word and the radio, we are still tuned to different frequencies and impressed with different word symbols, signs and images.

In many ways, we see ourselves, and hear and read of ourselves, through the images and reflections of others. We live in a history others have made or created for us. We echo sounds and display skeletons of empty structures. We are inheriting desert islands created for us by others. Our vision of our societies is created by foreign laws and cultures. Whether that vision is in accord with the gospel teachings, or with the vision our ancestors saw, is something we hardly find time to think about. We are so busy making patterns from a carbon copy that we often forget we too have the necessary tools to create new hopes and visions based on our ancient cultures and gospel teachings. . . .

The Secret of True Solidarity

There is indeed a great sense of unity already in the Pacific. Two foreign languages widely spoken among the schooled are English and French. In at least three Melanesian countries — Papua New Guinea, the Solomon Islands and Vanuatu — there is an even closer affinity brought about by the Pisin or Bislama language.

I believe there is more to Pacific solidarity and unity than I have sketched here. To my mind we must all be involved in the search for the creation of a new order. Because our nation-states and communities are still small, we can see the faces of people behind power structures. We can hear the cries and groanings of those who suffer from oppression, loneliness, illiteracy, disease, hunger, landlessness and ultimately, Godlessness.

We are like the new Jacob invited by old Esau to go on a new journey. We must respond with deep commitment to our God, for the "children are weak," and we must consider our people and their children's children. If our people are driven too hard against their souls and identity, they will die. We would like to call on our God, on our Christ and on our ancestors' wisdoms to go on ahead of us. We must move more slowly with our flock at their pace, until we are united on that eternal shore of the Pacific (see Genesis 33:13-14).

We must carefully and systematically identify values and virtues dearest to us. We must obey the basic laws of nature. We have to be quick to forgive and slow to be angered. We have to be quick to conserve our resources of fish, timber and natural environment, but slow to exploit for quick money. We should be careful to plan and live within our budgets and slow to promise illusory hopes to our people. We have to live by loving and hoping and not die by hating and despairing. We must live by courage and not by fear. We must live by cooperation and not tear ourselves apart with bitter competitions. We must live by our hard work and sweat and not by begging and depending on welfare or charity handouts.

Whatever talents we have are God's gifts to us. Even if we do go astray in abusing these gifts, we must not lose hope. For us to live is for us to hope. We must hope for a new future. Revolutions come and revolutions go, like tides and waves that ebb and flow. But the sign of hope is the only hope we have. In the Christian context, our common commitment to Christ is our hope for the new world we must build. The old states have perverted the Word of God and are creating death traps everywhere. We are members of the new world — the brave new world. Like our ancestors who crossed the oceans single-handed, we must take courage and build a new Pacific.

Unfortunately, many people today see the Pacific as a hideaway place. People like to go to the Pacific to laze under swaying palm trees and be entertained by lovely grass-skirted women or bare-chested boys. It is becoming a place for some to salve their consciences and do what they could not do in their own countries.

The Pacific is becoming a waste heap, a dumping place for all manner of filth and dirt. The destructive powers of science were released following the destruction of Pearl Harbor in Hawaii. Americans, French and Japanese continue to dump their waste in the Pacific. Recently the Chinese have joined their allies in dumping waste in the very fountains of our survival. Medicines that are certified as dangerous in some countries are sold in the Pacific to kill our people.

The Pacific must not be seen as a world of dreams inhabited once by gentle savages who are now happy to live under their thatched roof houses and watch the sun go up and go down, day by day and year by year.

I believe the secret to our solidarity does not lie so much in the creation of common Pacific-wide institutions like banks, shipping and airlines, in seminaries, universities or common markets. These are of course valuable institutions for unity. But the real solidarity must lie in our desire to create small Christian and human communities of villages, clans, towns, cities, offices and relationships. Creation of regional institutions will create centralism and bureaucracy unless heroic efforts are made to make these institutions responsible to the needs of our small people. I believe we must work toward creating small Christian communities and perfecting the communities God in his wisdom gave us through our ancestors. We must try to live as far as we can by the sacred charter of the Beatitudes.

I believe we of the Pacific have somehow to take up the candle, the burning torch, to the mountain of hope. We must rekindle our society with hope and insist that the success and progress of society must now be judged not by the number of warehouses for weapons, the number of soldiers and the gross national product, but by the steadfast adherence to the Beatitudes. We must become the wind and the current that diverted the oncoming storm. We must offer a new glimpse into old, wounded hearts for a new hope. We must build societies which are "more genuine, just, and taking root in sharing and love."

YUMI MAS TINGTING

CHORUS

Yumi mas tingting	*We all must think*
Se yumi ol brata	*All of us are brothers*
Everyone nomo	*Every single one of us*
Ol man New Hebrides	*We're people of the New Hebrides.*

VERSES

1. Kaontri blong yumi   *This country of ours*
   E mi gat tu kaf man   *It has two governments*
   Mekem man aelan   *They make the people of the islands*
   Karanke tumas   *Hopelessly confused.*

2. Skul I strong samting   *Education is a powerful tool*
   I lusum taem long yu   *It takes time*
   Be biaen long em   *But if you persevere*
   Bai yu klat tumas   *You'll be glad in the long run.*

3. God I wetem yumi   *God is waiting for all of us*
   We ples yumi stap   *In our various places*
   Wonem yumi mekem   *What we are going to do*
   Emi stap yet   *Remains to be seen.*

4. Sorry olgeta   *I feel for all of us*
   Yu falla I go nao   *You must now set to*
   Blong leftem ap   *And lift right up*
   NAME NEW HEBRIDES   *The name of the New Hebrides.*

5. We ples yu wok   *Wherever you work*
   REMEMBER NEW HEBRIDES   *Remember the New Hebrides*
   Yu pikinini   *You are the children*
   Blong New Hebrides   *Of the New Hebrides*
   Everyone nomo   *Every single one of us*
   Ol man New Hebrides.   *We are all New Hebridean.*

Kali Vatoko

Development Is People

Sitiveni Ratuvili

Development is people. Not people having things done for them. Development is people doing things for themselves. That is what governments and others often forget.

Three Basic Principles

We think there are three basic principles in development if it is to be relevant to the needs of the people.

We Must Use Our Own Resources. In many places the central government tries to do everything for the people. Sometimes the church does the same thing. They may even ignore the local resources which the people themselves have. Outside agencies come with their aid and development plans and impose them upon the people. This is bad for the people. It makes them dependent. They take the attitude that this or that development scheme is not their responsibility. So they sit back and wait for something to happen.

But development need not be imposed like this. There are many ways in which the people can be helped to develop themselves to become self-reliant.

In Indonesia a method of plowing before planting rice has been introduced that avoids the cost of introducing expensive machinery. The field to be plowed is covered with water and then buffalo are chased around inside the fence. This stirs up the ground and has the same result as plowing with modern machinery.

In Erromanga, in the New Hebrides, villages have recently built their own kindergarten. They did it with the materials around them that they normally use. Because they did it themselves, it was their own project. If an outside agency had built a "model" kindergarten it might have been modern and well-equipped. But it would have been imposed from outside. It would have encouraged dependency from the people and would not have been true human development.

It is therefore a basic principle that true human development looks first to the local resources which the people themselves have. For this is the way to build self-reliance instead of dependency.

We Must Be Aware. What do we mean by "awareness"? We are thinking of what Jesus was talking about when he spoke of people "who have eyes to see and ears to hear." That is what Jesus Christ wants of us all. He wants us first to have eyes to see and ears to hear what he is saying to the churches and to the world as a whole. And he calls leaders and ordinary people to understand the forces that affect their lives.

Government services are often too sophisticated. The people just do not understand what is being done. They are confused and frustrated because so many different things happen at once. One week there may be a visit from the Agriculture Officer. The next week the Education Officer will come, followed by the Health Officer. And so it goes on. Each of these is working independently, with no coordination.

In all this confusion the Christian minister has a role to play. He can help the people to be aware of their real needs and to understand the opportunities available. He can help them to become more aware. To do this the minister must be aware of the real needs of the people. He must see with his own eyes and hear with his own ears.

The churches in the Pacific are called also to be aware in another way. They must take a prophetic view of all that is happening in the name of "development." They must look critically at what is happening and see what is good and what is harmful. They must be able to see where outside pressures in development create false needs in Pacific people. For example, advertising creates consumer needs. People develop a taste for tinned fish and other packaged foods, when they live close to the sea and could be catching fresh fish.

Awareness leads people to realize when they are being manipulated. It can sometimes lead them to say "no," instead of, without thinking, simply saying "yes."

Christian awareness is seen in action when the people work together in the community for growth. And Christians should be encouragers. When a project is doing well, they should say, "That's a good idea."

We Must Face Up to Failure. Some attempts at development fail. We cannot help failing sometimes. People are like that. We do fail. But our attitude to failure matters very much.

Many organizations, including governments, find it difficult to admit failure. Even churches can be guilty of this. They feel they cannot afford to admit failure, because they may be criticized or lose the support of the people. They may also lose overseas support. So they persist with their mistakes until this brings tragedy.

But the Christian way is to admit failure. We should always be willing to look critically at what we are doing in our development projects. We should be willing to change what we are doing, if we have got it wrong. If we find we have failed, we should stop and learn from it, and then begin again.

Some Questions That Need to Be Asked

About Food. Villagers who live near the sea may prefer to eat tinned fish, even though they have made a good catch of fresh fish.

To be able to buy tinned fish in a shop is not good development, but bad. For tinned fish is less good for our bodies than fresh fish. It can even cause people to suffer from malnutrition. And they are poorer too. They have spent their money to get tinned fish, but fresh fish they could have caught free!

Other people eat too much heavy food and do not have a balanced diet. In many places the women and children suffer most, because it is the custom for them to eat last, after the men have taken everything they want. By then most of the good food is eaten. The children may fill their stomachs, but they have not had the good foods they need to make their minds and bodies strong and healthy.

The churches should be alive to problems like these. They should help people to understand the different foods which their bodies need, especially their children. We could stress the need for more community work. If the people work together they can help one another to grow more food and a greater variety of crops.

About Cash Economy. Pacific Islands as a whole are certainly moving now into a cash economy. People must pay money for what they need. Most Pacific communities are having to adjust to the rapid change in their lives in which goods and possessions are now valued in money. Some people have learned how to exploit this.

In Fiji, it has been said, it used to be possible to buy easily a good basket of kasava. Now, increasingly, market sellers put the big ones on top of the basket, but underneath is "rubbish." They find they can earn good money that way. But they are giving poor value. The customer suffers.

In the Highlands of New Guinea the wealth of the people is counted in the number of pigs they own. Once, after a big government function, where two-and-a-half-thousand pigs were killed and eaten, someone asked: "How much does this represent in cash?"

If one pig requires two years to raise, time is money. Two-and-a-half-thousand pigs, times two years to raise them, is a lot of time and a lot of money. The church and Christian people must work out the meaning of money and the place it should have in Pacific communities. It is a question of deciding what we value most. And it often affects traditional customs also, especially the exchange of gifts and such practices as "bride price."

About Political Action. The church in the Pacific today cannot avoid becoming involved in political action, in one way or another. It must happen, if the church is to be fully with the people at their point of need.

When we speak of political action we are not talking about party politics. Christians may give their support to a political party on a particular issue with which they agree. But the Christian stand should always be with the interests of the people rather than with a political party.

Christian politicians throughout the Pacific who put the interests of their people before party loyalty should be supported. It is difficult for politicians to remain true as Christians, because of the many pressures and temptations which they face. They need the understanding and support from church people to strengthen them. And if they fail to give their politicians this support, they should not complain too loudly if things go wrong.

Christian people can influence political decisions only if they are involved in the decision making of their communities and nations.

About Bride Price. "Bride price" is sometimes a problem in some places, for example, in Papua New Guinea and in the Solomon Islands. In the past, "bride price" was simply a way of giving gifts and of bringing two families together. But as people more and more want cash in the new money economy, "bride price" can become an excuse for greed.

The churches need to study more deeply the changing marriage practices and the dehumanizing effect these changes are having upon families throughout the region. In some areas many young people have decided to live together outside of marriage, simply because they feel they cannot afford the "bride price," or for some reason they are afraid to approach their families. Some couples in this situation try to conceive a baby in the hope that this may influence their families to permit the marriage. In other places women are dehumanized by the oppressive way in which wives are exchanged.

About Wantok. "Wantok" is a pidgin word for the ties which bind together members of a clan, a family or a language group. As we use the term "wantok" we are thinking not only of pidgin-speaking parts of the Pacific but of the extended family system throughout the region.

The concern which members of families or communities have for one another has always been a strength in the Pacific. But the custom has become a problem today for people who move from the villages to work and live in the towns. They are often exploited by members of their families who come from the village to stay with them. Both the town dwellers and the villagers have their own needs in this situation and both need to be understood.

The village people feel that those members of their families who are privileged to work and earn salaries in towns have a greater opportunity and responsibility to share what they have. They see the higher standard of living that their town relatives enjoy, and they feel the great gap between that and their own simple life in the village.

On the other hand, village people do not always realize the great strain that they can put upon their town relations. They do not realize that everything in the towns, including food, costs money, a lot of money. Town dwellers, for example, usually have no land nearby on which to grow their own food. They may have more money than their village relations, but they need more money too to maintain their life in the town. And we should not forget that some of the poorest people in the Pacific, who suffer the greatest misery, are those who have failed to succeed in the town and are doomed to stay there in the squalor of slums.

We believe that the government cannot solve cultural problems like this simply by passing laws. The problems are human ones and can only be solved by human understanding. The church stands closer to the people than the government and can help to detect exploitation. The church can also help the people to understand and cope with changing values, and can take a lead in helping to solve the great social problems in our towns and villages.

True Independence in the Pacific Islands

Walter Hadye Lini

I believe that the work of this Conference will be incomplete if we are to think that all we need to accomplish at the end of this Conference can be achieved by passing resolutions, by requesting financial assistance through the PCC and the WCC [World Council of Churches], and by dissemination of information through the papers, radio and other media just so that the world may know of our struggles.

If we believe this is all, then we have missed the most important accomplishment of this Conference. We would have returned home to our respective countries not knowing our visions and our final destinies. And we would have continued to busy ourselves in different strategies until we are old and dead. We would have deceived ourselves, and we would have believed that we had progressed, but in fact we would have stagnated, if not actually moved backwards.

True Independence Means Caring for Human Life

The most important achievement of this Conference is the genuine realization that the only true and genuine basis of independence for the countries in the Pacific is dependent on the type of love and care we give to human life, not political independence. This value and care of human life has been forgotten by the Western world. The West has completely destroyed the right of the people, and in particular small peoples, to be free, through unmerciful control of humans and avaricious efforts to subdue the earth. The people's right to manage their land, their culture and their whole way of life has been undermined. This has been done through physical and psychological genocide as in Australia and New Zealand, through physical slavery and through education and other institutions in other countries. The crushing of the authentic philosophy of life of the Pacific peoples has led to serious dislocation and the alienation of peoples one from another. Their democracy and their Christianity have contributed to this inevitable destruction. Admittedly, the churches have done a lot for us, but they must face the challenges of our rapidly changing times. It is heartening to note that the churches took an initiative to organize this Conference, out of which we have begun to feel and experience our common solidarity. This solidarity has long been denied us through natural ocean and land barriers and, more recently, through colonial divisions. Our common objective now is to work toward a common goal.

Toward a Common Goal

My vision for us is that we work toward a common goal. My vision is that we replace the Western assumptions—destructive values and void philosophies—with those of our people, in order for us to be authentic and independent peoples in the image of God. Our governments, churches and constitutions and the assumptions underpinning them must be challenged so that the dreams and hopes of our peoples about the kind of society we want will be realized. I would like to suggest that: a.) we choose a slogan for the Pacific; b.) we begin right away with requests to PCC, WCC and other funding agencies to see how we could move toward a new direction with our Pacific Island leaders; and c.) a conference be organized with the specific objective of developing our philosophy to restore our identity and solidarity, as soon as funds are available.

Our Island Heritage

A free society can only be governed with the trust and the consent of the people. Once that trust has evaporated, a government can only be maintained by coercion.

It is my considered opinion that if we are to avoid many of the social ills and evils which are now plaguing those societies and countries and which were bequeathed to us during our colonial years, if we are to avoid social injustice which will breed a lack of trust, then we have a duty to embark upon an examination of many of the alien attitudes and practices that at present exist in our countries. We must have the courage to acknowledge that the historical consequences of European rule have left us with attitudes and practices which stand in need of modification to local conditions. We have a duty to take steps to establish, and in some instances reestablish, values and practices that are best suited to the needs and ideals

of the people of Melanesia. It really is a question of attitude. Our national institutions must be geared and tuned to servicing and nurturing a social, political and economic order suited not only to our environment, but also within the limits of what it is possible for us to achieve: in short, an order that is in keeping with the expectations and needs of the people and not one hampered with the preconceived notions of a society that basically has little in common with that which prevails in the region.

The time to begin to decide the way in which such a society is to be formed and the nature of leadership required has most definitely arrived. As the social crisis in the Western world deepens and its leaders begin to speak of the need for their people to renounce the drug of an ever-increasing material consumption, the Pacific Island states could, in many ways, demonstrate that their indigenous values—and a practical reemphasis of them—serve as a very good and timely example. Indeed, a practical application of Pacific Island wisdom could well serve to give us an international distinction out of all proportion to our size and geographical location.

The Way to the Future

Furthermore, I suggest that to do so would be, ultimately, in the interests of our own social cohesion. Nothing destroys trust more quickly, nothing makes social division and unrest more certain than a national diet of failed expectations. Basically, we have to be sure of what we can achieve for our people, and if this realization means we restore some of our traditional concepts and values while retaining some aspects of the systems which were set down in our islands by the advent of European rule, then that is the path we should tread.

That it may be a difficult journey and one open to misinterpretation is not in doubt, but the people of the Pacific Islands enjoy a common heritage of courage and an ability to produce leadership which acknowledges that our various situations often require it. And as it has been in the past, so may it be in the future. Let us progress in our own chosen way, encouraged by our achievements of the past and inspired by the vision of the society that is our heritage and our bond for the future.

The Kanak Struggle for Independence

Yan Celené Uregei

The Kanak people has survived the holocaust of colonization and is, more than ever, determined to struggle to obtain their liberties and to exercise fully all human rights. The Kanak people affirms to the international community its desire to exist, to remain forever, as a people having an original civilization. It reddens the faces of the colonizers with its pains arising from the present practices of colonial genocide. It denounces the French colonial power in the Pacific. It denounces French capitalism and imperialism which lean on powerful military forces of both classical and nuclear kinds in the Pacific.

The international community has already declared the South Pacific a zone of peace. It will compel the colonial, military, capitalist and imperialist power to return to the Kanak people without delay the power for peace in this zone. For, in Caledonia, the only legitimate people is the Kanak people, presumed to want independence in accordance with international law of decolonization. [Eighty-two percent voted for Independence leaders; however, the Kanak people are in a minority in their own nation. French citizens, other immigrants and especially Indochinese refugees also have the vote.—Ed. note]

A Short Historical Summary

French colonial power took possession of the Kanak country by military force. By the decree of January 20, 1855, it declared itself the only owner of all the lands (this decree is still in force). The Kanak people (under Great Chief Atai) revolted against this theft of lands and their enclosure in ''reserves.'' Crushed, subjected [subjugated] and physically eliminated, there were only 26,000 people left in 1927 (from an original 200,000). As for the survivors, the colonial power carried out a policy of destruction of the Kanak culture.

In 1947, the deletion of New Caledonia from the UN list of nonautonomous territories was a unilateral and colonial act of France, for it was done without the agreement of the General Assembly of the UN and without consulting the Kanak people, which at that time did not have the right to vote.

The 1958 Constitution of France admitted the princi-

ple of self-determination of colonized peoples and the right to independence (being human rights). Article 76 authorized New Caledonia to retain the status of Overseas Territory. The Kanak people opted for this status with the guarantee of the French government that the government regime in Caledonia would remain that of the Cadre law with Kanak ministers (the aim of this law was to lead the colonies to independence). In addition, the 1958 Constitution, article 75, offered the Kanak people the guarantee of being able to live according to their own customs and to give life to their civilization. Indeed the Kanak people keeps an individual civil law, a distinctive sign of a colonized people.

Institutional Development in New Caledonia

The colonial power has by steps suppressed the Cadre law by applying the Jacquinot (1963), Billotte (1969), Stirn (1976) and Dijoud (1979) laws. The Dijoud statute suppressed the local government in the sense of the Cadre law. The colonial power has taken over exclusive responsibility for all economic, financial, mining and school matters, etc.

In place of the organization of the Kanak people into tribes with their own customary authorities, which were legally recognized under the regime of the Cadre law (a last step before obtaining independence) in force in 1958, a system of communes of the type existing in France was set up under the control and direct and narrow protection of the colonial state. The High Commissioner, appointed by the colonial power governor of Caledonia, carries out all the powers of the French government and chairs the Local Council of Government (elected by the Territorial Assembly) but has no power; he only has a role of leadership and supervision. The colonial power has at any time, according to its good pleasure, the right to suspend or dismiss the Council of Government (it did so at the beginning of 1979).

The Dijoud law is a departmentalization of Caledonia. This law just keeps the title "Overseas Territory" for motives of political opportunism with regard to the independent countries of the Pacific in particular. [A department is the approximate equivalent of a state in the United States or a province in Canada—Ed.] The real aim of the Dijoud law is the carrying out of a policy of integration with the ultimate purpose of destroying Kanak civilization—a retrograde policy condemned for many decades by the international community.

In the face of a colonial power which practices genocide, the UN is the only remaining guarantee of human rights, notably the right to self-determination and independence. In the South Pacific, the independent states in their meeting of the Forum in Honiara (Solomon Islands) in July 1979, strongly reaffirmed their "belief in the principle of self-determination and independence for all the peoples of the Pacific islands, including those of the French territories" and invited the French government to work toward this end.

The Kanak people, in the elections on July 1, 1979, voted en masse for the Independence Front (grouping together the five independence parties) which presented single lists of candidates for the local Assembly. The Kanak people's desire for independence has been clearly and continually shown since it obtained the right to vote. A not negligible number of votes from the non-Kanaks upheld the right to self-determination and independence of the Kanak people.

The Rise of Fascism in Caledonia

In order to dissolve the legitimate claims of the Kanak people, the colonial power practiced a policy of massive systematic immigration of population foreign to the Pacific. In the last ten years, it has installed 25,000 Europeans alongside the 55,000 Kanaks in Caledonia. This immigration, which had eased off during the last three to four years because of economic conditions arising from the nickel crisis (nickel is the main product of the Territory), has increased again, with the application of the Dijoud Plan, to approximately 1,000 immigrants a month. The colonial power has also installed Vietnamese refugees with a view to suppressing the Kanak people's right to independence.

In addition, the colonial power has available extremely large armed forces (military, gendarmes, police), and civil servants (in superabundant number), who owe it obedience and who have the right to vote in Caledonia.

The colonial power, through its policy of genocide by substitution, wants to apply the precept of majority rule (as it is practiced in an independent democratic country) to Caledonia, which is colonized, and to tell the international community that the people of Caledonia (and not the Kanak people) does not want independence. It is effectively easy for the colonial power, under the pretext of military maneuvers or other motives, to progressively introduce 10,000 to 30,000 more people—either military or police or civil servants—in order to drown out the votes of the limited numbers of Kanaks (55,000 souls).

The Kanak people, strengthened by the international community's support and its right, has demonstrated its desire for independence, despite the violent and wild repression of the armed forces of the colonial power, which did not hesitate in prohibiting peaceful political demonstrations.

The colonial power has favored the regrouping of former military and police personnel, who were previously in former colonies—Algeria, Black Africa, Indochina—and are now in Caledonia. Organizations such as the OAS (secret army organization) have issued death threats and will not hesitate to put them into action, killing the Kanak people and non-Kanaks supporting independence.

Some Europeans, colonists in Caledonia who are in agreement with capitalism and multinational corporations, do not hesitate in asking for independence for Caledonia. However, at present no political party has been created in this direction. This independence would be of the neocolonial kind, allowing France to continue plundering and wasting the mineral and maritime resources of the Kanak country.

French imperialism has already been demonstrated in the Pacific with the unilateral creation of a 200 sea mile economic zone. Thus France has become the third largest maritime power in the world. In a neocolonial independent Caledonia—directed by Europeans and former colonists, with the support of a few Kanaks—French imperialism would impose a regime of government which favors itself.

Economic Plundering by French Capitalism and Imperialism

In its 126 years of domination and exploitation, the colonial power has introduced wild capitalism in the Kanak country. It has stolen the land and the natural mineral, maritime and energy resources to distribute them gratuitously to the local capitalists (exclusively European). The colonial state has also become the major industrial capitalist (with the Societé le Nickel), the major financier and banker (Societé Generale, Credit Lyonnais, Banque de Nouvelle-Caledonie, etc.) and is also an international company (multinational company SNEA), with close connections with IMETAL, BP, etc.

Thus the colonial power and the local capitalists have plundered and wasted all the resources and have accumulated immense profits. The colonial power, as administrator of capitalism, has itself created all the conditions of the economic crisis and has led workers to unemployment. (The large majority of Kanaks are unemployed and return to life in the "reserves," or reservations.) The capitalists continue to amass large profits, even in the time of crisis, which they then export and no longer invest in the Territory. Despite this major unemployment, the colonial power has introduced immigrants and provided them with work, to the detriment of the unemployment already in Caledonia.

Since the French army took possession of the Kanak country, the Kanak people has been put in "reserves," national land of the colonial state allocated provisionally to the indigenous people who were in the process of disappearing. In the "reserves," the Kanak people has maintained its civilization, its customs, its traditional culture. It has survived, despite genocide, by practicing subsistence farming (yams, cassava, taro, bananas, etc.) on poor land and mountainsides.

The colonial power has used this colonized people for the construction of roads and collective installations, through forced labor, to obtain the big triumph of the European colonists and wild capitalism. Thus the Kanak people has been worked at the pleasure of others. With the stopping of forced labor and the acquisition of the right to vote, the Kanak people has remained the "labor reserve" or the unemployed of capitalism triumphant or in crisis.

Basically, the Kanak people is a people of peasants. The colonial power did not concern itself with the improvement of conditions of land, work tools or lodging of the Kanak people; in a word, it took no interest in the improvement of the living conditions.

In all centers where the colonists live, material and technical progress has been made for the immediate profit of the colonists. The standard of living of the Europeans in New Caledonia is one of the highest in the world. During this time, the Kanak people lives in daily misery in the "reserves," where there is the highest level of unemployment, where there is lack of arable land—

not enough to sustain the indigenous population which has now noticeably increased.

In the Kanak country, the colonial power has practiced a policy of affluence in the extreme, to the exclusive profit of the Europeans, and a policy tending to lead to the destruction of the Kanak people (the infant mortality rate is high, etc.). It is clear that this is a "French-style apartheid" policy in the South Pacific, aiming at eliminating the Kanak people from its own country. The colonial power seeks all possible means to get rid of the Kanak people's claim for independence.

To Build a Multiracial, Fraternal, United Society and Socialism

The Kanak people has always had one civilization. It calls for the immediate application of the right to self-determination and independence in order to be able to live its civilization fully and to put a permanent end to the genocide practiced by the colonial power. All non-Kanak workers introduced into the Kanak country have the right to be different; on the day of independence they will have to opt either for Kanak citizenship and nationality or they will retain their national status without change. Thus every immigrant worker will have the freedom of choice.

After the choice has been made, all citizens will have the same rights, the same duties, and will enjoy all liberties; human rights will be exercised under the guarantee of the Kanak state.

To avoid the tragedies of colonization, the Kanak people believes that it is time to draw lessons from the history of decolonization. It beseeches the colonial power to put an end to genocide and to guide its nationals on the path of independence of the Kanak people, without trying to set up neocolonialism in all its forms or a French-style Rhodesia.

The Kanak people wants peace in order to build and consolidate a multiracial, fraternal, united Kanak state and socialism, where the people will have regained all their land and will have nationalized all its natural resources, means of production, etc. The whole people will then have put an end to the social relations of domination engendered by capitalism and will have replaced them with egalitarian relations. They will form, together with other peoples, notably those of the Pacific, an anti-imperialist front to oppose the actions of multinational corporations and those governments which support them.

LAND

Doomed to eternal torture
I cannot bear it any longer
To see you scalped and raped
By earthlings and nonentities
See how they lacerate you
And incapacitate you
Violate your person and
Suck life out of you
Yet you suffer in silence
The indignity of castration
Total annihilation and
Gradual descent into nothingness

But your plea is crystal clear
Your conditions are simple
You don't want a concrete forest
Infested with subhumans
With the noose around their necks
You want to bargain life with life
You have a fertile womb
Ever ready for the act of procreation
Adam was your offspring
But has divine sanction
To commit incest
Till you enfold him once again
In the embrace of death
While in transit.

Sitiveni Ratuvili

Independence and the Kanak Peoples of New Caledonia

The Evangelical Church in New Caledonia and the Loyalty Islands

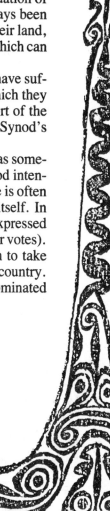

In their meeting at Goaru Houailou, August 27-31, 1979, the forty-five members of the Synod unanimously declared themselves for the accession to independence of the Melanesian (Kanak) people.

• The Synod studied the past and present situation of the Melanesians in the country. They have always been the occupants of the country and are one with their land, and by this right they are the only ethnic group which can legitimately claim its independence.

• The Synod recognized the injustices they have suffered and the open and hidden oppression to which they are subjected today. The gospel calls for support of the oppressed—that is the main explanation for the Synod's decision.

• The Synod does not ignore the good that has sometimes come from the new occupants nor the good intentions of France, although behind the words there is often a vacuum. But that would not be sufficient in itself. In the election of July 1, 1979, the Melanesians expressed their wish for independence (82.5 percent of their votes). They now have a majority which enables them to take charge themselves of their own life in their own country. They can no longer accept being helped and dominated by others taking responsibility in their place.

PART FIVE:

GLOBAL ISSUES FROM A PACIFIC PERSPECTIVE

Editor's Note: Two of the three selections that follow are by authors who have served the churches of the Pacific and are advocates for justice for Pacific Island brothers and sisters.

James Winkler's article about economic injustice speaks mainly about the controlling interests of Asia and Australia/New Zealand in the Pacific Basin. However, we can also see the complicity of North American interests. Winkler has served the Pacific Conference of Churches as a mission intern through The United Methodist Church, U.S.A.

The selection from the 1978 Ponape Conference on a Nuclear-Free Pacific outlines the involvement of the United States, France and the USSR in nuclear activity in the region, over which Pacific Islanders are becoming increasingly incensed.

Father William Wood's testimony before the Trusteeship Council brings us full circle to the possibility of our involvement as United States and Canadian citizens in advocacy ministries on behalf of Pacific Island concerns. Father Wood chairs the Micronesian Action Working Group of the National Council of the Churches of Christ in the U.S.A.

The poem by Joe Murphy again raises for us the intense frustrations of Pacific Island people over their constant manipulation at the hands of developed nations. Murphy is a member of the Micronesia Support Committee in Hawaii.

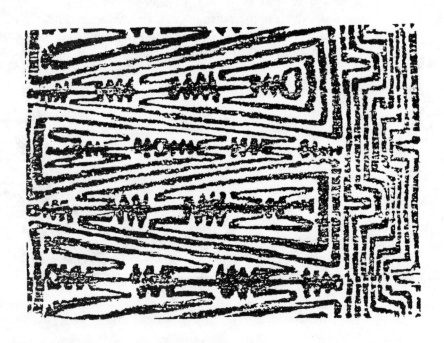

WE DO NOT WANT NUCLEAR WASTES DUMPED IN OUR OCEAN.

WE DO NOT WANT THE TESTING OF NUCLEAR BOMBS

WE DO NOT WANT NUCLEAR-POWERED SHIPS PASSING THROUGH OUR WATERS

WE DO NOT WANT TO BE DEFENDED WITH NUCLEAR WEAPONS

WE WANT A
NUCLEAR FREE PACIFIC

Pacific Conference of Churches

1. The Pacific Conference of Churches makes a strong statement on nuclear issues in this poster.

2. Ghostly reminder of World War II points up the urgency of the quest for peace today.

United Methodist Board of Global Ministries by John C. Goodwin

United Methodist Board of Global Ministries by John C. Goodwin

3. Pollution is increasingly a problem for Pacific Islanders.

4. Multinational corporations, represented here by a Dutch and British petroleum company and a Japanese-made car, play a controversial part in the economy of the Pacific.

5. James Winkler (R), whose article appears in this section, chats with the Rev. Albert Burua of the United Church in Papua New Guinea and the Solomon Islands.

Clashing Interests in Pacific Development

James Winkler

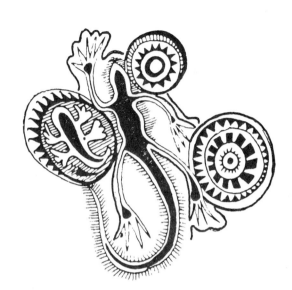

The Pacific seems to live up to its name. It appears to be a peaceful place. Dramatic visible expressions of violence are not widely found.

Yet in its own way the Pacific is rapidly becoming an arena of intense competition, conflict and struggle. Its eco-system is in danger of irreparable harm. Its cultures, rich in values, are being eroded, some of them undone. For those who view human life in its wholeness, who see humans in relation to their community and culture and in intimate relation to their ecological context, this raises fundamental human rights questions.

These are the opening lines of a statement adopted by the Fourth Assembly of the Pacific Conference of Churches in Tonga in May 1981. Powerful countries and corporations, at the expense of the ocean and the islands, the people and the future of humanity are thoughtlessly seeking to satisfy their insatiable hunger for material resources and for control. The economic model which current trends represent comes from the outside and is inappropriate for the Pacific Islands. Long

popular but under increasing attack in the West, it centers on narrow economic goals and carries with it unacceptable costs. Pacific Island nations generally find themselves dependent for economic planning and management upon persons and organizations who do not recognize these realities or who feel unable to cope with them. This means there are many points at which the interests of Pacific Islanders and powerful countries and corporations come into conflict.

The Pacific Basin Cooperation Concept (PBCC) being promoted by Japan with the ready support of the United States and Australia, and less enthusiastically by some others, represents an unfortunate reinforcement of existing relationships of power and control. Endorsement by the Pacific Island nations is now being sought for the PBCC as a means of "legitimizing" the scheme in a psychological/political sense. The process is well-lubricated by a multitude of new aid offers.

The Pacific Basin Cooperation Study Group, appointed by the late Japanese Prime Minister Ohira,

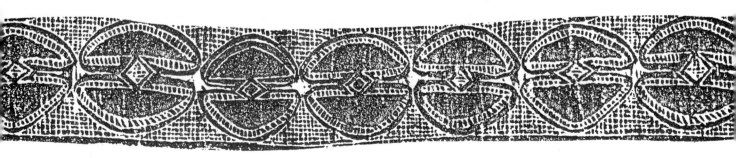

recommends the advancement of a number of "noncontroversial" projects such as cultural exchange programs, increased tourism, internationalization of Japanese universities, cooperation in resource exploitation, a "Pacific Basin Industrial Policy Consultative Forum" and a "Pacific Basin Declaration on Trade and International Investment." Japan, Australia and the United States see the PBCC evolving over the long term.

The idea of a PBCC has not originated solely in government circles. A number of organizations such as the Pacific Basin Economic Council (with a membership of over 400 companies) and the Pacific Trade and Development Symposium have played crucial roles supporting the PBCC since the 1960s. The Nomura Research Institute (Japan), the Brookings Institution (USA), the Australian National University and the New Zealand Institute of International Affairs are a few of the "think tanks" that are part of the process of shaping the PBCC.

This reveals the way in which the complicated "root system" of transnational corporations (TNCs) has extended into universities, research institutes, governments and lobbies to influence governments, foundations, industrial organizations, influential upper classes and even churches.

"Exchange programs," "internationalization of educational and research institutions," "development of tourism," "cooperation in resource exploitation" need to be looked into with extreme care by the small nations. Pacific Island nations may have to face the reality that while they may like to avail themselves of the capital and the technology of the larger nations, their long range values and interests may be shared less by the larger countries and corporations around the Pacific Rim than by other small Third World countries, even those far away.

The coming of deep-seabed mining brings a new kind of competition and unknown dangers for the ocean, with benefits to Pacific people as yet unclear.

After many years of negotiations, the agreement reached at the Law of the Sea Conference in 1980 is in trouble due to the Reagan administration's decision to "review" U.S. policy. United States military and industrial strategists would like the mineral riches of the seabed to be exploited for their own benefit by transnational corporations with a minimum of international controls. Five major consortia of corporations have been formed for the purpose of mining the seabed, and have invested hundreds of millions of dollars in the necessary technology. A few of these companies are: British Petroleum, Rio Tinto Zinc (U.K.), Mitsubishi (Japan), U.S. Steel, Lockheed Missiles and Space (U.S.), INCO (Canada), Societé le Nickel (France) and Royal Dutch Shell (U.K./Netherlands).

Under the proposed Law of the Sea agreement, an International Seabed Authority would be established to govern and administer mining of the seabed; revenue-sharing of seabed mining would be guaranteed; and an international mining venture called Enterprise would carry out mining in addition to mining by private companies.

There are three major areas in the Pacific Ocean where the potato-shaped nodules containing manganese, nickel, copper and cobalt are found in abundance. One area lies between Hawaii and California, another in French Polynesia and a third between Hawaii and Micronesia.

The proposed Fiji Development Plan 8 (1981-85) includes a provision for an Industrial Free Zone (IFZ):

> The main objectives of setting up an IFZ during D.P. 8 are to develop industrial land for export-based industries only and to administer this as a free zone. . . . Such industries are assembly-type operations and are generally labor intensive.

An Economic Development Board is being established to facilitate this process. The 1980 report of Fiji's Central Monetary Authority states that:

> Foreign investment would be welcomed and encouraged by various means including provision of appropriate incentives such as tax holidays, tariff concessions, accelerated depreciation allowances, export rebates, etc.

Given the experience of other nations with Free Zones (also known as free trade zones and export processing zones), serious questions are raised in Fiji's idea of a Free Zone.

There are currently about eighty Free Zones in various parts of the Third World, the majority in Southeast Asia (Taiwan, South Korea, the Philippines, Malaysia, Singapore and Indonesia).

Free Zones depend on foreign investment, although typically host governments provide the land, buildings, power and water, and insure that the labor will be cheap and union-free. The Free Zone is separated from the rest

of the country by barbed-wire-topped fences and patrolled by zone police who search employees as they leave. Sovereignty is virtually surrendered to the foreign investors as there are usually no corporate income, property and excise taxes, and no import quotas or duties.

The Free Zones in operation have more often than not provided less employment than was anticipated. In fact, unemployment may have increased as many laborers from rural areas have headed to Free Zones in hope of finding jobs. Employment levels in Free Zones have fluctuated considerably as transnational corporations use inflation, recession and the offer of better deals from other Free Zones as reasons for laying off workers or moving out. Capital-intensive technology is rapidly making many jobs obsolete. One motive for developing Free Zones is the hope that technology and knowhow will be transferred to the developing country. This has not proved to be the case, as most jobs in Free Zones are broken down into the simplest tasks possible, and managerial jobs are predominantly occupied by expatriates. Basically, the Free Zone distorts the economies of developing countries and represents an ill-fated attempt to become integrated into the international economic system on an equal basis.

A shipping registry or flag-of-convenience law and a tax-haven have been established by the government of the newly independent nation of Vanuatu. The tax-haven status brings more than 600 foreign companies and banks to Port Vila to take advantage of the tax-free provisions and secrecy afforded by the tax haven. The Melanesian International Trust Company Ltd. advertises:

> There are no income, salaries, profits, corporate, sales or withholding taxes and, with the exception of certain local land transactions, no capital gains taxes. Additionally, there are no gift, estate or succession duties. Stamp Duty is levied on certain instruments and documents affecting property or interests in Vanuatu. Vanuatu has not entered into any tax treaties or double tax agreements with other countries. No exchange controls operate on foreign currencies in Vanuatu.

Vanuatu allows corporations to register their names and maximize their profits by selling their goods at a low price to their Vanuatu subsidiary and reselling them at normal or higher prices in another country. Thus, Vanuatu is complicit in and legalizes the efforts of these corporations and banks to avoid legitimate taxation and public scrutiny in return for a small fee.

Similarly, the new shipping registry or flag-of-convenience law allows shipping companies to avoid taxation and safety regulations, and to operate with cheaply paid, nonunion labor. Again, Vanuatu appears to become an accomplice in abuses by business in return for a small fee.

New Caledonia is the world's second largest producer of nickel, most of which is exported to Japan. The Evangelical Church of New Caledonia reported to the PCC Assembly: "*It is often said that New Caledonia is nickel.*" The nickel industry is in the hands of a few miner-settlers and one large French company, the Societé le Nickel. Each 25,000-ton boatload brings the miners 28 million francs. Fifty percent of the population — mainly Europeans — benefit from this industry. The other 50 percent suffer from its effects.

The privileged place of nickel has meant that few other sectors of activity have developed. The consequence of this has been that the territory has been susceptible to the fluctuations of the international nickel market, and in order to provide supplies and equipment, New Caledonia has become increasingly dependent on the outside.

Societé le Nickel's smelting plant in Noumea is currently running at about 60 percent of capacity. Paul Bliek, SLN's manager, has pointed out, "When we have problems, New Caledonia has problems."

Foreign investment in the Pacific Islands has been dominated, historically, by Australian- and New Zealand-based capital.

The names of two of Australia's biggest corporations, Burns Philp and W.R. Carpenter, are familiar to most Pacific Islanders, although they may not be aware of how many other companies are controlled by these two, often jointly. (In fact, Burns Philp is one of the 20 largest shareholders of W.R. Carpenter.) The total investment these two companies have in the Pacific Islands is unknown. Both Burns Philp and W.R. Carpenter may have Pacific Island investments exceeding 50 million Australian dollars, perhaps up to 100 million. Pacific Island operations provide well over half of W.R. Carpenter's group profits and a sizable portion of Burns Philp's profits. Until recently, Burns Philp derived the vast majority of its profits from its Pacific Island operations, but during the 1970s, BP embarked on a course of rapid expansion into the Australian market. This strategy was of course largely funded by profits from the Pacific Islands. Burns Philp has not chosen to pull out of the Pacific. On the contrary, the past several years have witnessed a spate of takeovers by BP.

Burns Philp and Carpenter have monopolized numerous sectors of Pacific Island economies. They are involved in trading, plantation agriculture, motor sales, manufacturing, hotels, insurance and shipping, among other things. They also derive power from their role as import agents. Some of the factors contributing to their success are: their long experience in and detailed knowledge of the Pacific Islands economies and national elites; the relative lack of competition they face (successful entrepreneurs are often bought out or driven out of business while potential large scale rivals usually choose not to compete due to the small markets and economies of the Pacific Islands); they have made full use of the linkages between their interest in plantations, insurance, trading, hotels, shipping, etc., and their close relationships with Australian banks and financial institutions.

The PCC statement goes on to say:

The forces now determining the direction of the lives of Pacific people come largely from outside. They may seem impersonal in nature, but they represent collective vested interests of very real persons and groups. We recognize that sometimes Pacific people and their leaders unwittingly become allies of these undesirable forces. We are often too easygoing, too comfortable, not critical enough about what is happening to us. Sometimes we are more interested in the "progress" of members of our own family than in the well-being of our country and region.

We ask our Pacific Island people and leaders to join in working for a clearer understanding among Pacific people of what is happening in this region; for critical self-examination; for a clarification of national and regional goals; for a reaffirmation of Pacific values.

Nuclear Arms in the Pacific Islands

Ponape Conference on a Nuclear-Free Pacific

An assessment of the nuclear weapons situation now, the new weapons systems under development and the meaning of these policies for us now and in the future is necessary so that we can develop strategies to oppose them and work toward a nuclear-free future.

Summary of the U.S. Nuclear Posture in the Pacific

The United States has between 8,000 and 12,000 nuclear weapons stored or deployed in the Pacific, compared with 7,000 in Europe; yet in congressional discussions much more attention is paid to the militarization of Europe than to the militarization of the Pacific. The 8,000 to 12,000 nuclear weapons include the following:

Fifteen hundred tactical nuclear warheads are aboard the U.S. Pacific fleet. In the U.S. Pacific Fleet, there are 122 ships capable of carrying and firing such nuclear weapons. These ships include aircraft carriers, cruisers, destroyers and hunter-killer submarines. A tactical nuclear weapon is defined militarily by the range of the weapon delivery system. It is not a small weapon, as is generally thought. Strategic weapons are long range weapons, such as B-52 bombers, land-based Intercontinental Ballistic Missiles, or submarine-launched ballistic missiles. They have a range of thousands of miles. Tactical weapons have a shorter range. They are carried by fighter jets and other kinds of shorter range vehicles for several hundred miles. The explosive power of many of these tactical nuclear weapons is as large and in some cases larger than that of strategic weapons.

At present there are 528 strategic nuclear weapons aboard seven to eleven Polaris-Poseidon submarines. The number of these submarines varies. Depending on the time of year, some of them are relocated to the Atlantic or other areas. A minimum of 3,000 nuclear weapons are stored in the Hawaiian Islands, all on the main island of Oahu. Other major storage and deployment areas for the United States include Guam, the Philippines and Okinawa. Of the 8,000 to 12,000 nuclear weapons in the Pacific, there are approximately 60 different kinds in the different delivery systems. They range from the ballistic missiles carried by bombers and submarines to such things as nuclear artillery shells, depth charges and torpedoes. Many people are not aware of the wide range of nuclear weapons.

The home base for Polaris-Poseidon submarines is Hawaii, with forward bases in Guam. The home base for Trident will be in Seattle. The forward base may be Palau because of its deep water port. Tridents have a much longer range than Polaris-Poseidon. With its most advanced missiles, the Trident will have nearly three times the range of Polaris-Poseidon, which means that it will be able to operate in an area of the Pacific three times greater than the Polaris-Poseidon submarines.

Concerning aircraft, the U.S. Navy has 108 nuclear-capable planes, called Orions, which are antisubmarine aircraft, in the Pacific. In addition, there are 576 aircraft carrier-borne planes. The U.S. Air Force has major bases in Hawaii, Japan, South Korea, the Philippines, Taiwan and Guam. The U.S. Air Force is equipped with several types of nuclear-capable aircraft, including F-111s, F-4s and A-7s. These are the shorter range aircraft. There are approximately 75 to 100 B-52s, strategic long range bombers, located in Guam. The U.S. Army has nuclear weapons in Hawaii, South Korea and the Philippines. It is more difficult to get exact numbers for Army nuclear weapons because Army delivery systems are not as easily identified as Navy or Air Force systems, but it is reported that approximately 700 Army nuclear weapons are located in South Korea.

That's a rundown of the weapons systems. In addition to the actual weapons and the delivery systems, there are other essential support systems that are tied directly onto operations of the weapons. There are subsystems, such as surveillance, command, control communications and navigation systems. All of these are present in the Pacific as well and make up a vital link of the nuclear weapons system. The most important communications are very low frequency systems, located in Australia, Guam and Hawaii. Navigational systems for nuclear weapons systems are located in Australia, Samoa, the Philippines, Japan, the Antarctic and Hawaii. The major U.S. Command Center for the Army, Navy and Air Force are all located in Hawaii. The commander-in-chief of all U.S. military forces in the Pacific is also in Hawaii. The U.S. Pacific Command covers an area about two-thirds of the world's surface and about the same percentage of the world's people. Its range extends from the West Coast of the United States to the East Coast of Africa and from the North to the South Pole. It is the largest military command in the world.

Important Developments

A very important development is the work being done in the field of the accuracy of these weapons systems, not only for the Trident missiles but also for the cruise missiles and the new MX missiles. All these systems are being designed to have an accuracy of within 100 feet, even when they are fired from thousands of miles away. This means that from 6,000 miles away the missiles can be fired into a room. It appears clear that this concentration on technological developments for precision accuracy is so that the United States could destroy Soviet land-based missiles while they are still in their silos. To destroy missiles while they are still in their silos would

mean that the United States would be launching its weapons first, because there is no sense in destroying silos if the missiles are not in them. So this whole move forward toward accuracy in U.S. weapons is a move toward a "first-strike policy"—a policy of making the United States capable of initiating a nuclear attack. (There is the case of an engineer who had been working with Lockheed, the number one U.S. military contractor. He worked for years designing the Polaris-Poseidon missiles and then Trident missiles. He resigned recently because he saw the United States developing this first-strike policy.)

Another development is qualitatively improving the number of warheads on each missile. For example, each Trident submarine will carry 24 missiles, and each missile will have 17 separate nuclear weapons, each going to a separate target. One Trident submarine will be able to destroy 408 cities. This is a fantastic force.

French Nuclear Activity in the Pacific

The 1979 French military budget was more than $12 billion according to the studies done by the French administration, which meant that they increased the 1978 budget by $211 million. One-third of this budget was for nuclear equipment. It proposed to raise defense credits 52 percent through 1982. The Ministry of Defence said that the revision of the military program to the year 2000 includes new nuclear and conventional weapons such as the Mirage 2000 jets. These plus the new nuclear submarines and other members of the new generation of tactical and strategic weapons are a factor which will correct the most flagrant insufficiencies in the French defense and attack system.

In September 1978, sixty dignitaries from Tahiti were invited to France. In France, they visited nuclear submarine bases. In 1980 the French government designed a nuclear submarine base to be built in the Marquesas Islands.

The USSR

Much less information is available concerning the USSR's nuclear weapons systems, but it is clear that the Soviet nuclear presence in the Pacific is limited to its fleet. There are roughly 105 Soviet submarines located in the Pacific and of these, approximately 40 are nuclear powered. (The others are diesel powered.) They also have 60 surface ships that have nuclear capability. All these ships have their home port at Vladivostok. At this time, they are based mainly in the North Pacific because of their shorter range delivery systems.

In addition to their weapons systems, the Soviets are doing nuclear testing within 400 miles of the Cook Islands.

U.S. Irresponsibility and Obligation in Micronesia

William T. Wood

In 1979 we stated our belief before the Trusteeship Council that the United States had not fulfilled its obligations assumed under the Trusteeship Agreement to promote in an appropriate manner the political, economic, social and educational advancement of the people of Micronesia. At the same time we urged this Council vigorously to exercise its responsibility. In particular we asked that the 1980 United Nations Visiting Mission pay close attention to, among other things, the degree of economic dependence that the United States administration had created, the social problems resulting from that economic dependence and the long term United States presence, the appropriateness of the educational system which has been developed by the United States in the Micronesian cultural context, the degree to which the United States administration of the proposed economic assistance package during the transition period was used to control negotiations in the fundamental areas of security and sovereignty and the problems arising out of the nuclear testing in the area.

At the same session of the Trusteeship Council, Professor William Alexander, speaking for the International League for Human Rights, also a member of the Executive Board of the Focus on Micronesia Coalition, called upon this Council to sponsor a comprehensive analysis of the state of the Micronesian societies. The purpose of the suggested study was to determine what changes have occurred in Micronesian society during the trusteeship period under the United States administration and to identify the problems the Micronesians face presently and would face in the posttrusteeship period. Information from such a study was seen as crucial to evaluating the extent to which both the United States as Administering Authority and the Trusteeship Council as monitor of the United States role in Micronesia had fulfilled their obligations. Also crucial was the improved understanding of their own situation which would be gained by the Micronesians from such a study. Only such understanding would ensure a truly free and informed choice regarding their future status.

In 1980, we returned to this Council with the same conviction. The United States had not fulfilled its obligations assumed under the Trusteeship Agreement. Furthermore, we stated that many of the problems of Micronesia arose as by-products of the American administration. On the other hand, it was also clear that the United States would continue to achieve its chief objectives, including strategic denial of Micronesia to other countries, even beyond the termination of the trusteeship. . . .

Now in 1981, we return once more to this Council. We

reiterate: the United States has not fulfilled its obligation to promote in an appropriate manner the political, economic, social and educational advancement of the people of Micronesia. In fact, the United States has created in Micronesia a distorted economy which continues to this day to impede progress toward self-sufficiency.

The political realm is strongly influenced by the severe economic dependency. As a result, even though political structures are in place and functioning for self-government, the possibility of truly independent choices is brought into question. Less evident, but just as real, are the failures in education. The educational system was modeled on American institutions and has produced graduates who are capable of entering the government bureaucracy and the teaching profession, but otherwise are not properly trained to contribute to solving the long range economic and social problems of their own people.

Finally, the recent emergence of serious social problems such as suicide, alcohol abuse and violence can be attributed to the past 15 years of United States-induced rapid transformation of the traditional culture and value system.

Now in 1981, we can say further that the terms of the proposed Compact of Free Association and the accompanying subsidiary agreements, which have been initialed by all parties to the negotiations, ignore to a large extent this legacy of unfulfilled responsibilities. Furthermore, the terms of the agreements appear to release the United States from fulfilling its original obligations while at the same time they guarantee that United States strategic interests in the islands will be well protected.

With these results, we must also question today whether the United Nations Trusteeship Council has fulfilled its obligations to the people of Micronesia. In the past, requests from our Coalition and other petitioners that this Council intervene more vigorously with the United States on behalf of the Micronesians apparently have not been implemented. The above-mentioned suggestion for a United Nations commission study to assess the impact on Micronesia of the United States administration and to identify some of the clearer implications of that history for future development in Micronesia was not considered seriously. The lack of such a study seriously jeopardizes the ability of the Micronesians properly to inform themselves and thoroughly to consider the implications of the unprecedented choice before them.

Settlement of the war claims of the Second World War and speedy implementation of laws regarding the destructive legacy in the Islands of nuclear testing have not been insisted upon by the United Nations. And now, when a Micronesian status of less than total independence is being considered, the United Nations apparently is content to observe the plebiscite at the request of the Administering Authority rather than actively to supervise this plebiscite and the political education process that will precede the voting.

If the United Nations does not act as advocate with and for the Micronesians, what can possibly counterbalance the clearly far superior bargaining power of the United States? The Coalition respectfully asks this Council to take time in its deliberations to consider fully the question: have we done all in our power to ensure that the United States took adequate steps to promote the political, economic, social and educational advancement of the peoples of the Trust Territory or have we served merely to legitimize United States self-interested activities in the Trust Territory?

The amount of time remaining during which the Council can have a positive impact on the future of Micronesia is unknown. The process toward a 1981 or early 1982 termination date may well have gone too far to reverse or postpone even if such a reversal or postponement were desirable. The fact that the new United States administration has not seen fit to complete its policy review of Micronesia in time to present its decision to this Council is a major handicap. The Coalition is distressed that this decision of the United States not to decide, greatly limits the ability of the Council to speak to the significant issues raised by the present initialed Compact of Free Association and the subsidiary agreements.

The 1980 United Nations Visiting Mission noted that:

> . . . even sophisticated Micronesians were for the most part woefully ignorant about the steps leading to termination of the Trusteeship Agreement, and appeared to be equally ill-informed about the political options open to them, including the terms of the draft compact of free association being negotiated by their leaders with the United States Government.

Now, a year later, little has been done to change this situation. The very least the Trusteeship Council should do is insist that the people of Micronesia have sufficient time and resources before a plebiscite date is set, in order to study and comprehend fully the implications of the unique political status, the development questions associated with the economic plan, the extent of authority given the United States in the area of defense and security, and the substantial limitations on the terms of the Compact contained in the subsidiary agreements.

We again request that the United Nations sponsor a study which would assess the impact on Micronesia of the United States administration and identify some of the clearer implications of that history for the political, economic, social and educational development of Micronesia over the next 15 to 30 years. Only in this way will the basic human right of the Micronesians to a truly free and informed choice be protected.

ON THE 18th OF APRIL

On the 18th of April in '62
With a fresh wind blowing, and skies of blue
The Pres approved memo one-forty-five
And the Solomon Committee sprang alive.
Eight summers ago—in '63—
Nine men came out from the Land of the Free
To the sunny trust isles, facts to find—
As well as assess the islanders' mind.

Their search was simple—just find what's right
To insure a favorable plebiscite,
And see that the long-shelved Micro-nation
Would be American-owned by affiliation.

Yes, out they came, these nine great guys
To serve as the President's personal eyes
And determine which way the natives would go
When the status winds began to blow.

The objectives were stated as a, b, and c
And were geared to do everything rapidly.
Their outline proclaimed that the Trust Islands' fate
Could be sealed and delivered by late '68.

Their final plan was really quite simple,
And resembled the act of picking a pimple.
After starting a TT-wide Congress as head*
They fill it with loads of Commonwealth bread,
And when it gets soft and ready to flow
They pump in some plebiscite fever and blow.

The name of the game was "Follow the Leader"
And the Solomon crew swore nothing was neater.
They also suggested that leaders be caught
By leadership grants and to Washington brought.

And even commented that kids in school
Could be curriculated toward American rule,
Adding that scholarships in gay profusion
Could win the voters through confusion.

To top this off, they said PCV's**
Will teach "The West" for chicken feed,
And a dash of Social Security, please
(To replace the function of coconut trees)
Will guarantee, without a doubt,
That Micronesians won't get out.

Joe Murphy

*TT: Trust Territory
**PCV: Peace Corps Volunteer

From *Micronesia Support Committee Bulletin*, vol. 6, no. 1 (Spring 1981). Used by permission.

PART SIX:

A PACIFIC POSTSCRIPT

Editor's Note: To understand the full dimension of Pacific Christian concern it is important to listen to a respected voice of Pacific leadership. Leslie Boseto from the Solomon Islands is such a leader. He led the United Church of Papua New Guinea and the Solomon Islands for the decade of the 1970s. He was so respected in his nation that he was the first choice for governor general when the Solomon Islands gained independence in 1977. (He chose, nevertheless, to turn down that possibility and to remain moderator of the church.)

The Fourth Assembly of the Pacific Conference of Churches spoke to the world. It had some definite things to say to the churches of North America. These statements are introduced by a short excerpt from Dr. Edwin Luidens's letter to Dr. Claire Randall, general secretary of the National Council of the Churches of Christ in the U.S.A., after his return from Tonga in May 1981. Dr. Luidens heads the East Asia and South Pacific work of the National Council of Churches.

The closing poem by Kiam Cawidrone is a fitting conclusion for a notebook of Pacific voices. When Pacific people sing out strong their keynotes are always in the solidarity of love.

1

2

1. *"Sing out strong . . . in the solidarity of love."*

2. *Blowing the conch shell, a peculiarly Pacific means of communicating.*

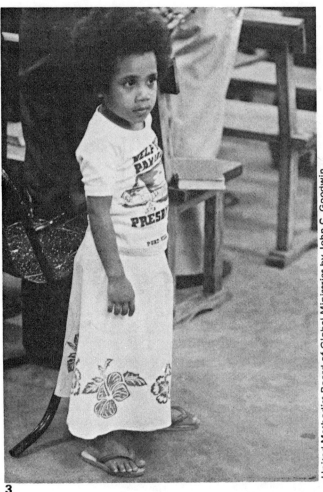

3

4

3. *Our challenge is to prepare our children for the world they will inherit and to leave them a world worth inheriting.*

4. *The Rev. Leslie Boseto, Bishop of The Solomon Islands Region, United Church of Papua New Guinea and the Solomon Islands, and the Rev. Joshua Daimoi, leader of the Evangelical Alliance of Papua New Guinea.*

THE CHALLENGES OF THE 1980s AND THE PACIFIC CHURCHES

Leslie Boseto

I have been asked to speak on the broad theme of "The Challenges of the 80s and the Pacific Churches." However, before I go on to talk about this subject, let the grace of God challenge this gathering so that we do not just see each other in the artificial and temporary classifications of our world's economic, political, educational, cultural and religious systems. I pray that this Assembly will not just be another mere gathering, but a starting point for liberating and reconciling gathering. So often in a gathering like this we talk a lot and end up piling up our reports with very little or no action at all. So the first challenge comes to us here and now: to look at each other and accept each other as all members of the human community, with common needs, common problems, common concerns, common desires and common struggles.

Whether we belong to an academic community or transnational community, industrialized community or rural community, chief-ly or royal community, religious or denominational community, we have the same human flesh and human bones. We have the same five classical senses. Naked we came into the world and naked we leave the world. Hence, we need each other with meaningful purpose and aims in life, not through the artificial covers of our modern world's bureaucracy's classification of human beings, but face to face with one another as true human beings.

Dr. Kosuke Koyama says: "Bureaucracy is a world of filing cabinets and endless classification. It can reduce a living person into a set of numbers one sees on his or her passport." If this Assembly is sincerely and honestly to face and combat the challenges of the 1980s, every one of us here must be liberated from our mental classification of participants in our cabinets of titles, positions, qualifications, orders, sexes and ages. Let us be more human than artificially human! I know that because of language problems and maybe the problems of our cultural identities, we may have some conflict over how to dress or what sort of food we like to eat or whose accent is French or English, etc. However, God came to the human community in Jesus Christ. He lived beyond human languages and human customs, beyond any religious and

political leadership codes and any royal structures and any legal rights and any economic systems that existed in his days. His language is love. His program is himself, with the oppressed, the outcast, the captives, the poor, the sinners, the sick. His power is forgiving love which always gives hope. For it was God in Christ who said: "Father, forgive them; for they know not what they do" (Luke 23:34, RSV).

As we look more closely at our subject, let us not forget that any theology the Pacific community may desire to let the wide world become aware of must be the theology of the love of God in our community and from our community. It must not be a mere and cold love which is forced by the availability of money or the world's bureaucracy's filing cabinets' expectations. It must be a real love which embraces the newborn babies and nurtures them in our homes until they are picked up by the scholarships of our nations! It must be a real and responsible love that feeds, clothes and shelters the school-leavers and dropouts whom we call the unemployed. Pacific communities, I believe, have been self-reliant for many thousands of years by the grace of God before the capitalists' philosophy was introduced. Do you also believe this?

The Challenges of the 1980s

I believe that the challenges of the 1980s are the same challenges that Moses faced in Egypt about 1400 B.C. And those who knew about him and his brave leadership wrote:

> It was faith that made Moses, when he had grown up, refuse to be called the son of the King's daughter. He preferred to suffer with God's people rather than to enjoy sin for a little while. He reckoned that to suffer scorn for the Messiah was worth far more than all the treasures of Egypt, for he kept his eyes on the future reward (Hebrews 11:24-26). The same challenge came to Jesus of Nazareth from Satan, who said: "All this I will give you if you kneel down and worship me." Jesus faced the same challenge from one of his confessors, who said: "God forbid it, Lord! That must never happen to you" (Matthew 16:22, TEV). Again he faced the challenge when Pilate used his legal rights and said: "You will not speak to me? Remember, I have the authority to set you free and also to have you crucified" (John 19:10, TEV).

The same challenge came in the time of Paul when he said: "Watch out for those who do evil things, those dogs, those men who insist on cutting the body" (Philippians 3:2, TEV). Again Paul said:

> For we are not fighting against human beings but against the wicked spiritual forces in the heavenly world, the rulers, authorities, and cosmic powers of this dark age (Ephesians 6:12, TEV).

It is true that we live in the world, but we do not fight from worldly motives. The weapons we use in our fight are not the world's weapons but God's powerful weapons, which we use to destroy strongholds. We destroy false arguments; we pull down every proud obstacle that is raised against the knowledge of God; we take every thought captive and make it obey Christ (2 Corinthians 10:3-5, TEV).

So, before we go on, I would like this Assembly not to beat about the bush or the brick-walled castle when we talk about the challenges of the 1980s. Let us first of all identify the challenger. The challenger is sin in our own hearts. It is sin of greed and selfishness in our social structure. It is sin of deception and hypocrisy which often is worn by our human society. People today have begun to talk a lot about "structured sin" or "sinned against." Are we free from within ourselves and from within the structured sin of exploitation, classification and discrimination?

It is now clear that before we talk about the challenges of the 1980s, we must first of all be freed from the side of the challenger. Because, says Jesus, "No one can break into a strong man's house and take away his belongings unless he first ties up the strong man; then he can plunder his house" (Mark 3:27, TEV). So, if sin is within us and within the comfortable structure of our society, it does not like to be challenged.

Our Regional Context and Our Communal Solidarity

The Pacific is the largest ocean in the world. Yet population-wise, we are very much in the minority, in small groups of islands many hundreds of miles distant from one another. Apart from the problems of communications, the Pacific region challenges us with its vast spaces of sea and air for nuclear testing and nuclear dumping by powerful nations. Why didn't God, at the beginning, give the Pacific Ocean to the present powerful nations? It is too big for our population to look after it. But can a purely technological community look after the Pacific Ocean? Can the efficiency of technology efficiently look after our marine resources?

But the Pacific Ocean is not merely sea. It is part of our human environment. It must be cared for by our own population, whether we are in the minority or the majority. It must not be taken by the powerful nations as an ocean without people. The nuclear testing that is being carried out in French territory, the proliferation of nuclear weapons by the United States government in Hawaii and other parts of the Pacific, the recent testing of nuclear ballistic missiles by the Chinese government and the use of our Pacific Ocean as a dumping ground for nuclear waste—all these are challenging threats to our scattered minority population. But we are not a minority here. Do you know that it appears that those whose environments have been technologicalized [sic] from their dependence are no longer dependent on the power of human love and human sensitivity and human ability? This is where I see our communal solidarity must be strengthened to challenge any artificial, institutional community which only builds its security on temporary and unstable fearful hearts by using technology for its defender!

Our theology must be the expression of God's gift of our communal society and this communal responsibility. The ultimate power, which no one—no power in heaven and on earth—will be able to destroy or defeat is love (Romans 8:35, 37-39). I am sure that love for one another—for the jobless, the school-leavers, the old people—is here with us. We may theologize this love and call it divine love or everlasting love, suffering or unconditional love, and so on. Whatever the Western theologians may try to search out for its meaning and interpretation, we know what they are talking about in their preaching and lecturing. It was here with us before Abraham was born! It is love that the economic systems of our time reject. It is human love that our technological world belittles, lessening its power. It is human love that bureaucracy fences around with its legal criterion and classification!

The gospel of the kingdom of God to us, then, is not something you look for from ''more qualified'' theologians or bishops and archbishops or popes and so forth, to tell us more about. No. It is already present with us, although we can never fully realize it until Christ is fully recognized in our midst. But who is to tell us that Christ is already with us? Who is to recognize him for us? The theology of communal solidarity must be developed; it has already been the basis of our communal society and responsibility in the Pacific. The words of Jesus which say, ''Foxes have holes and birds have nests, but the Son of Man has nowhere to lay his head,'' are more understandable to the members of our Pacific society, which depends on the mercy of relatives or villagers, than to the industrialized society in which each individual member is dependent on a money economy and hence on the availability of employment. Therefore, the nature of the struggle of a society based on a monetary economic system is competitive and exploitative. And it creates the ''theology of vandalism,'' as one of our Melanesian leaders discovered.

Because of the vastness of our ocean and the small dots of islands, we must develop a theology of the communal solidarity of human society within the region of the Pacific. This theology of communal solidarity must begin from within each local and national context. Each national context must be our definition of our local church. The universal Christ who is the head of the church can only be recognized as universal when the people of God in every national context are touched by his forgiving love, and hence are very sensitive to where God's Holy Spirit is at work in their midst and through them. The Christ of the church and of the world can never be merely imposed organizationally and institutionally as universal. He must be experienced as he is, always ready to be personally invited, not impersonally enforced!

The Pacific Island nations will never become superpowerful nations in terms of military supremacy. However, we can become superpowers in terms of communal solidarity within our communal society of human relationships.

The Church in the Context of the 1980s

First, contextual challenges of the 1980s will increasingly be insecurity and fear expressing themselves in different ways and forms. Some of these expressions will be wars, some will be the search for more space and peaceful areas such as our Pacific region to be places for getting rid of dangerous wastes from what were believed not to be dangerous things twenty to thirty years ago. Some of these expressions of insecurity and fear will be seen in the way thousands of people look for employment. Governments of the day will use their power to cover up and get rid of justice, love and truth by murdering or detaining or exiling those who are and will continue to be brave in unmasking sins of injustice, hatred and deception. This fear and insecurity will also express itself in an attitude of not favoring decolonization.

Second, contextual challenges of the 1980s are increasingly ''loneliness'' and ''meaninglessness.'' Greed and the abuse of technology means rich persons can be surrounded by expensive furniture, television sets and one or two well-fed dogs, but have no friends and even be strangers to their neighbors. This spirit of loneliness may not yet be experienced in our communal society in the Pacific region. However, let us not be blind, because we have been hooked or chucked into the international economic system of the world. And I have no hope from any theology developed from Western experience and understanding of loneliness which will help us in the Pacific and also help us to freeze out and change the international economic order. We are probably the only segment of the world who still has hope for the liberation of the whole world! The theology of time, leisure and extended family responsibility must be developed and examined in the light of the Kingdom's gospel of communal society, which was first experienced on the Day of Pentecost in a new way. It must be sharing community that we develop—sharing between people, not between business companies.

Here is what Kosuke Koyama said in the Melbourne Conference on ''Your Kingdom Come'' about the meaninglessness of life in this age of technology:

We appreciate technology. How could we do so many good things in the sight of God of the Bible today without the help of technology? Technology may be permitted to duplicate anything, but not human beings. The machine must be switched off when it begins to duplicate the image of God in humans. It must not desecrate the holy in people. The world of efficiency—the world of attractive hands—must be watched by the world of meaning—the world of mutilated hands. What does it mean to duplicate human beings? Today perhaps one could speak of the duplication of the human in the sense of biological science. But I am thinking at this moment of surrendering of human space and human time to the efficient technological space and technological time. When the human environment is thus technologized, the uniqueness of the person will eventually suffer, and there will appear a faceless mass of people. The crucified Christ challenges such a technologically efficient way of dealing with people. Technology must serve the maintenance and development of human values of sincerity and reliability in the human community. The lifestyle of the Atlantic world is not the standard for all humanity. It must be judged together with other lifestyles under the light of the crucified Lord.

There are a lot of questions we can raise from the above quotation to discuss in this Assembly: What is the place and role of technology to develop human values? What is our Pacific understanding of the covenant God and hence the community-creating God in our communal society in the Pacific? To what extent will we surrender our Pacific-ness of human space and human time to the efficient technological space and technological time? How can we go about unhooking ourselves from the lifestyle of the Atlantic world in order to globally share and recognize our communal solidarity? What is our understanding of the term "crucified Christ" in our Pacific context?

The third contextual challenge of the 1980s is religious movements. In the Pacific context, the challenges of small movements who confess the same Lord and Savior appear to be increasing. The influences of world religions like Islam, Hinduism and Buddhism will increase through our business and cultural relationships. The traditions of our so-called established churches, unless they are open to both the judgment of God and the direction of the Holy Spirit, will continue to be defensive for their self-centered, clerical and male-dominated organizations.

The call is not so much church unity but Christian unity. All Christians in the Pacific context must take seriously the unity of all Christians in a given national context.

Christ Himself Challenges the Churches in the Pacific

First of all, this Assembly must examine what we really mean by the "churches." When we talk about "churches," we seem to take for granted that because of their established and registered status in our island nations and because they have been with us a long time, therefore we can naturally accept their organizational, doctrinal and theological identities. And thus, so often, we indigenous leaders of the churches in the Pacific have been mentally injected to believe that our denominational cultures or identities are all "eternal." Therefore, all we need to do is simply help our own denominational members to be better Methodists, better Anglicans, better Roman Catholics, better Baptists, better United Church members, better Lutherans and so forth. Those who have been Methodist-ized, Anglican-ized, Roman Catholic-ized, etc., must always be supporters and maintainers of their organizational programs and be sure they attend the right church buildings on Sunday. If the prayer of Jesus in John 17:20-23 has not been really obeyed by the believers in Christ's name, then Christ continues to challenge our divided church. The world is getting stronger and stronger and the divided church is getting weaker and weaker. So we are challenged by Christ to witness God's community for mission in the world.

Second, Christ challenges our institutional churches where the ordinary people, the poor, the oppressed are. Jesus is always at the side of the unprivileged, the oppressed and the least in our society, while we church leaders and church-paid workers continue to manipulate and exploit those who are under our oppressive structures. The gospel for the poor, for the dropouts from the educational system, that we preach from the pulpit Sunday after Sunday is not gospel at all! Our words are full of hypocrisies and lies! Jesus challenges us that we are hypocrites. Christ always moves toward the periphery. He was born and crucified outside Jerusalem.

Third, Jesus challenges our narrow views of his gospel. The king of the kingdom is multidimensional. He is both the messenger and the message of the kingdom. Dr. Mortimer Arias points out the many ways we tend to reduce the kingdom of God: to a transcendent kingdom which has nothing to do with the realities of history; to the church and church expansion; to the inner realm of religious experience; to an apocalyptic kingdom beyond history, leaving no hope for the present; to a new social order, identified with a particular ideology; and to a present kingdom of euphoria without tension and groaning for the final liberation of all creation. "Any one of these 'reductions' of the kingdom is a legitimate aspect or dimension of the kingdom announced and inaugurated by Jesus, but the problem is that we pretend that our favorite 'reduction' becomes the whole of it," he says.

Christians in the Pacific are challenged by the one who came to give life in all its fullness. It is not one-quarter of life that Jesus came to give, not even half or three-quarters of life but the wholeness of life. How often are we in the Pacific passively used to becoming mere carbon copies of what others in other countries and regions of the world feel, even believing that their special reductions are the wholeness of the gospel of Jesus Christ?

Fourth, Jesus stands revealed and challenges us with his love. Because of his love there is no longer a place for the devil to stand hidden. Jesus stood untouched by the law and even challenged the administrator of the law to accept that his authority to administer any good law was only given to him by God. People continue to search for further hiding places in this planet earth and in other planets. But Jesus Christ stands alone to challenge us to stand with him as we face the future responsibly. How often we try to challenge our people, yet we stand in hiding places of our employment, privileges, position, etc.

Last, Christ challenges us for not seriously witnessing the gospel in its urgency. The church-centered and Sunday-centered and minister-centered church program will never take seriously the urgency of the gospel of salvation. Do you know that Satan is happy when he sees that we are absent and fail to recognize and locate where he really operates? He also is very capable and cunning to use us church leaders for his own ends.

The lay people who are full of the Holy Spirit have begun to challenge our ordained ministry, which usually confines itself within the doctrinal and traditional expectation of the churches. In many cases, the lay people save more souls for Christ outside of church buildings and Sunday services than the ministers who are enslaved to traditional preaching from brick-walled buildings do. Therefore, the lay people today are more aware of the Holy Spirit and also the urgency of sharing and witnessing the gospel of Jesus Christ than those of us who are busy with interiors of church buildings and weekly programs. They are more like the Good Samaritan and we are more like the levites and priests! The lay people have come to identify some dead logs from the ordained ministry. You may not believe me, but I speak from what I know. It is the lay people who are daily encountering the realities of the world. Therefore, the question of the urgency of evangelizing the world through lay ministry is imperative and in the long run is not expensive and exploitative.

Conclusion

This Assembly must not beat about the bush when we want to be obedient to the call and command of the king of the kingdom, Jesus Christ, in order both to face the challenge and to be with Jesus Christ where he is being born and crucified. The Good News of the kingdom calls for total repentance. In calling the churches to repentance and restructuring in mission, the Melbourne Conference said:

We must affirm that the Crucified Christ not only challenges the structures of society, but also institutional churches' structures. An effective response to this challenge is crucial to the fulfillment of the mission entrusted to the church by the risen Christ. It calls for repentance and restructuring.

Churches are tempted to be self-preserving, but are called to be totally committed to the promises and demands of the kingdom of God. Churches which are tempted to continue as clerical and male-dominated are called to be living communities in which all members can exercise their gifts and share the responsibilities. Churches which tend to be decaying or morbid and form stifling structures are called to be living communities in which all members can exercise their gifts and share the responsibilities. Churches are tempted to be exclusivist and privileged but are called to be servants of a Lord who is the crucified Christ who claimed no privilege for himself but suffered for all. Churches tend to reflect and reinforce the dominating, exploiting structures of society but are called to be bodies which are critical of the status quo. Churches are tempted to a partial obedience but are called to a total commitment to the Christ who, before he was raised, had first to be crucified.

Therefore the Christ of the kingdom, who is already in the 1980s context, challenges the churches holistically to repent and to restructure in order to be worthy channels and witnesses of the kingdom.

The Mind of the Pacific Churches

Edwin Luidens

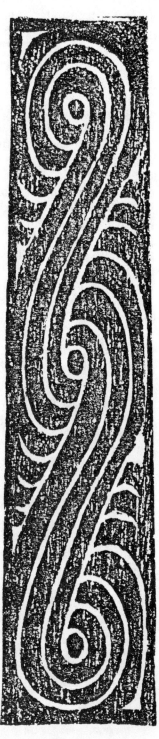

Pacific Islanders are involved increasingly in taking control of their own destiny. This dynamic process is increasingly aggressive, which does not mean it is military or strongly confrontational. However, this assertiveness causes them to experience more vividly the forces opposing them. How long they will contend in a nonviolent "Pacific Way" for their own aspirations and rights depends on how frustrated they become with external forces when such forces are not reasonably responsive.

The fact that any of the major powers could reduce them to nothing by military action leaves them undaunted because it seems morally unthinkable and probably politically unacceptable. By the sheer force of moral and humanitarian values, they challenge the superpowers to abandon the use of nuclear force, at least in their region, and to cease even atomic testing and nuclear dumping in the Pacific. They expect brother and sister Christians in the West to stand with them against the principalities and powers from outside the Pacific, just as they call on one another to act with greater coordination to deal with those forces within their region dehumanizing their own people. The dynamic interplay of differing kinds of power in the Pacific region should make the next decade lively and challenging for them and for us.

Editor's note: *The following selection, from the Secretariat of the Pacific Conference of Churches, highlights events at the Fourth Assembly that relate particularly to North Americans.*

To the Churches of North America

Nuclear Issues. The Assembly reaffirmed its commitment to a nuclear-free Pacific, adding:

As Christian people committed to stewardship, justice and peacemaking, we oppose and condemn the use of the Pacific for the testing, storage and transportation of nuclear weapons and weapon delivery systems; the disposal of radioactive wastes; and the passage of nuclear powered submarines and ships.

We recognize the intimate relationship not only between the development of nuclear energy and the problems of radioactive waste disposal, but also with nuclear weapons proliferation. We therefore object to further development of nuclear power until the problems of waste and proliferation are convincingly resolved.

Further, as Christian people we are concerned about the colossal investment required for nuclear armaments and nuclear power, and urge the investment of our limited resources toward total human development, particularly for poor and rural communities, and for alternative safe and renewable sources of energy.

Colonialism and Neocolonialism. Resolved:

In the Pacific sin comes in many forms. The church must take a firm stand against it in the name of truth. An ecumenical theology must not be afraid of criticizing evil in all its forms, without exception.

We request national churches to make reports and recommendations on...the situation of Aborigines in Australia, Maoris in New Zealand or Melanesians in Irian Jaya, or the neocolonialism in newly independent states, or Australian political and economic domination of the South Pacific Forum.

Special Concern for Decolonization in New Caledonia. Resolved:

That independence for the Melanesian people of New Caledonia is in line with the aspirations of Pacific people for self-determination and we therefore support them in their struggle.

That we urge our Pacific governments to play a helpful role in this process, including the effort to return New Caledonia to the United Nations list of countries to

From the Fourth Assembly of the Pacific Conference of Churches, Tonga, May 1981

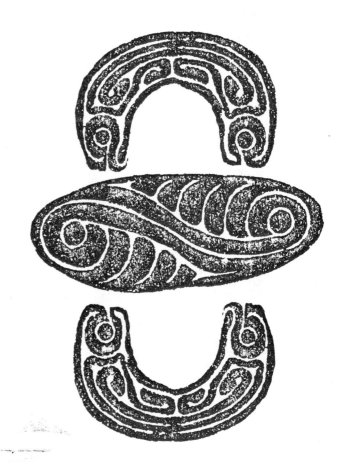

which the "Declaration on the Granting of Independence to Colonial Countries and Peoples" applies.

That we request the Government of France to immediately stop its policy of encouraging the immigration of people of other races into New Caledonia, further increasing the marginalization of Melanesian people in their own land.

That we express our concern that in the emerging nation of New Caledonia there be justice for all persons, and that the rights of minorities be protected. . . .

Special Concern for Micronesia. Resolved:

We are concerned about the denial of basic rights to the people of Micronesia. The United States of America was charged under the United Nations Trusteeship Agreement to "protect the inhabitants against the loss of their land or resources" and "protect the health of the inhabitants." However, U.S. activities have revealed a lack of commitment to the true self-determination and integrity of the Micronesian people. We hope that an impartial evaluation and a vigorous constructive debate may take place both within and outside of the United Nations to help clarify the basic relationships now being confirmed in Micronesia. We encourage the churches to support activities which will help the people to be aware of what they are voting for in the forthcoming plebiscite on political status.

Trade, Dependence and Powerlessness. Resolved:

That we give more attention to the question of how we in the Pacific might work toward a society of peace, justice and sustainability.

That there be a continuation of the studies of transnational corporations by the PCC Secretariat. . . and that the PCC Secretariat keep itself informed about Pacific Basin Cooperation developments.

Tourism.

That the PCC join with the Christian Conference of Asia, the Asian Catholic Bishops Conference and the Caribbean Conference of Churches to be founding members for an ecumenical coalition on Third World Tourism. . . .

Women in Decision Making.

We believe that Pacific women today are becoming increasingly aware of their need to participate in all aspects of the life of the church and society. We feel that the question of the place of women in church and society is seen increasingly as a question of development and justice.

We strongly recommend that:

—a women's staff person be appointed to the Department of Justice and Development;

—the PCC officially request the member churches and councils to increase the participation of women at all levels;

—the PCC Executive Committee include at least one woman;

—the PCC delegation to the World Council of Churches Assembly in 1983 include at least one Pacific woman.

Electronic and Print Ministries of the Church. Guidelines:

We encourage the use of satellite media. . . .

With regard to radio ministry, the prime targets are rural people, youth, people not working, those who don't go to church and non-Christians.

PCC (should) assist national bodies to set up local structures capable of developing film libraries when appropriate. . .coordinating with International Catholic Film Association and UNESCO. . . .

Committees [should be appointed] to. . .prepare material for publication by Lotu Pasifika Publications. . .to combat evil practices in the society and for submission as appropriate to the relevant countries who are causing all the trouble and danger in the Pacific with the production of nuclear trade and other

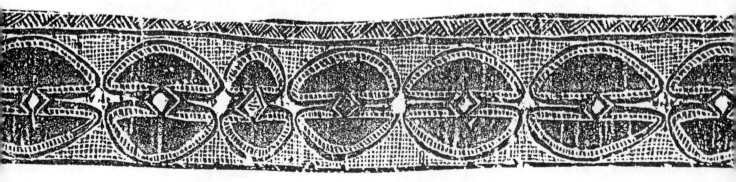

issues. . . .

We recommend that PCC encourage the Lotu Pasifika Publications to undertake the publication of materials in different languages on various subjects. . . .

Family Life—Youth Group Report. We urge all member churches:

—to encourage a style of family life in which young people share more with their parents in communication and decision making;

—to build active concern for young people and their needs into all its programs;

—to consider the special needs of young married people;

—to work with governments on the value of traditional skills and patterns of life;

—to see that there is a place for Christian consideration of politics within their life and programs.

Ecumenical Sharing of Resources and Personnel.

Sharing in mission from place to place, island to island and nation to nation has been from the coming of the gospel and continues to this day to be part of the way of our Pacific churches. As such we see the following:

—That the role of PCC then should be to encourage and support the intranational and international movement of personnel, resources and thought concerned with mission throughout the Pacific and perhaps beyond.

—That PCC encourage and give assistance to the member churches so that they may, in conjunction with their related churches, mission boards and agencies, take this sharing as a matter of priority for mission in the 1980s.

Funds [should] be set aside from money given from within the region by related churches and agencies to facilitate ecumenical sharing of personnel within the region.

PCC [should] play a major role in drawing to the attention of church leaders. . .the challenges of the universal and international mission of the church.

This Assembly requests member churches to inform their related churches, mission boards and agencies of these resolutions.

Visits of the National Council of Churches (U.S.A.) Travel Seminar (1982) and the World Council of Churches Ecumenical Team (1983).

Purposes of Visits:

—to hear what Pacific people say;

—to be with them;

—to share with them.

Regional concerns for observation and discussion:

—Nuclear-Free Pacific

—Independence of New Caledonia

—Tahiti

—Irian Jaya

—Timor

—Transnational Corporations

—Theological Education

—Tourism

—Migration

—Pacific Basin Cooperative Concept

We urge that the U.S.A. visits should be seen as part of the preparation for the WCC Assembly.

Values and Gifts of the Pacific Peoples. Considering ways in which they could participate uniquely in the universal mission of the church, the Pacific participants offered this list of values and gifts:

—the ability to harmonize our culture with Christianity;

—a self-sustained life style in harmony with the environment;

—strong Christian commitment, offering themselves in God's service;

—generosity and hospitality;

—cheerfulness and enthusiasm;

—celebration.

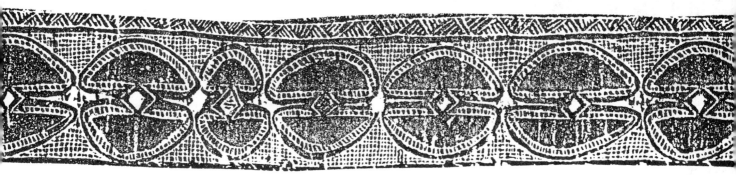

LOVE

Brothers and sisters of the Pacific
If you have a hole in your life
Fill it with Love

Old, young, adolescents
If you have a vacant moment
Fill it with Love

Love whom you can
Love when you can
Love all what you can

But...Love always!

Do not think — I am afraid
Do not think — I am ashamed
Do not think — I have my doubts

Go with the strength you have

Go simply
     lightly
     gently

          in search of Love.

Kiam Cawidrone

From *Youth*, vol. 4, no. 1. A World Council of Churches publication. Used by permission.